Peter Graystone is Assistant Director of Discipleship and Ministry for Southwark Diocese. In that role he helps Christians in south London live out their faith with confidence and understanding. Formerly he worked for Church Army, establishing projects that take the good news of Jesus Christ to people who are unaware of how much they are loved by God. Over the years he has also worked for Scripture Union and Christian Aid. He has been a Reader at Emmanuel Church, South Croydon, for over thirty years, preaching and leading worship. He is a speaker at the Greenbelt Festival, presents *Pause for Thought* on BBC Radio 2, reviews theatre for the *Church Times* and has written more than twenty books. He has also created the website <www.Christianity.org.uk>.

THE BARE BIBLE

Uncovering the Bible for the first
time (or the hundredth)

Peter Graystone

First published in Great Britain in 2018

Society for Promoting Christian Knowledge
36 Causton Street
London SW1P 4ST
www.spck.org.uk

British Library Cataloguing-in-Publication Data
A catalogue record for this book is available from the British Library

ISBN 978–0–281–07843–1
eBook ISBN 978–0–281–07844–8

Typeset by Manila Typesetting Company
First printed in Great Britain by CPI
Subsequently digitally reprinted in Great Britain

eBook by Manila Typesetting Company

Produced on paper from sustainable forests

For David

Contents

1 How to start

Don't start at the beginning. Trust me. Don't!

The Bible is a huge book. It's in two volumes. They are called the Old Testament and the New Testament. The word 'testament' is no longer used very often, except in someone's 'last will and testament'. It means, very loosely, settlement or deal, but that's a poor indication of what it implies in the Bible about the rich, glorious gift of God to humankind. If you approach the Bible expecting to discover what that gift can do for you, I can tell you without hesitation that you will uncover life-changing things.

The Old Testament is the older of the two volumes and it is revered as a holy book by both Jews and Christians. It tells the story of God's dealings with humankind over many hundreds of years until about the fifth century BCE (or BC, as Christians would say – Before Christ).

The New Testament tells the story of Jesus Christ, the founder of the Christian faith, and the beginnings of the Church in the years that followed his life, death and resurrection. It records events in the first century CE (or AD, which is the abbreviation for *anno domini*, a Latin phrase meaning 'in the year of the Lord'). Most of it was written during that century too, very soon after Jesus lived.

So why am I urging you not to begin at the beginning? The Old Testament is chock full of wonderful stories, and they are well known. It has the story of Noah, for instance, whose ark can be found in every toy shop, and Joseph, who had an amazing technicolour dreamcoat. Parts of it are a joy to read.

But in all honesty, some of it is a slog. There are long lists of names of people who have been forgotten by history. ('The sons of Lotan: Hori and Homam. The sons of Shobal: Alvan, Manahath, Ebal, Shepho and Onam.' Yup, page after page! You'll only enjoy this if you are looking for a unique baby name and you don't mind the child never forgiving you.) There are rules that would have been vital to life in a desert 40 centuries ago, but now seem completely obscure. ('Do not cut the hair at the sides of your head or clip off the edges of your beard.' Take that, hipsters!) And there is a lot of war and bloodshed which you can't ignore because it did actually happen, but is absolutely not what the Christian faith is about.

My suggestion is that you start reading the Bible with the New Testament, because that tells you precisely what the Christian faith is founded on. Start with the story of Jesus Christ. Come back to the rest – it won't go away – but begin with the story of the person who is such a monumental figure in the unfolding of life on earth that time itself is measured in relation to him: BC and AD.

I was once at a party where I met the chief executive of a company that publishes Bibles. She was very charming and the food was amazing, so I took courage to pitch an idea that I thought would secure my place in history. I suggested that she published a version of the Bible in which the New Testament came before the Old Testament. That way people who had never read it before would plunge straight into the life-enhancing teaching of Jesus. They wouldn't give up 100 pages into the Old Testament when confronted with exhaustive details of how many tassels there should be on a priest's undergarments.

She looked at me like I was a crackpot. I lost heart, excused myself and stood in the kitchen with a sausage roll.

So now that opportunity has been lost for ever, I am going to suggest the second best option. Open a Bible about two-thirds of the way through. Start to read at the New Testament. In my opinion this is one of only two works in the history of culture where the sequel is better than the original. (The other one is *Toy Story*.)

Look for a book with the title 'Matthew' (or 'The Gospel According to Matthew', or something similar). It's one of four biographies of Jesus that begin the New Testament. One of the many surprises of the Christians' holy book is that, despite being regarded as the greatest person in the history of humankind, Jesus did not get a section of the Bible named after him. In fact nobody knows precisely why the names Matthew, Mark, Luke and John became associated with the biographies. They've been the titles of those books more or less since they were written, however, so it's reasonable to guess they were the names of the authors.

Matthew, like all the other books that make up the Bible, is divided into chapters. They are indicated in the text by large numbers. And each chapter is broken into segments indicated by smaller numbers – one or two sentences in each. These are called verses.

Chapters and verses were not part of the original text, but they're now accepted worldwide as the only way to find your way round. So Matthew 11.28 means Matthew chapter 11 and verse 28. That verse is a tremendously attractive promise of Jesus which has given hope and heart to people for centuries in their times of need: 'Come to me all you who are weary and burdened, and I will give you rest.'

It's hard to imagine how Christians ever managed without these divisions into chapters and verses, but for many hundreds of years they did. It was an Englishman who had the brainwave about chapters at the beginning of the thirteenth century. His name was Stephen Langton, a priest who had been elected leader of the Christians of England (a post known as the Archbishop of Canterbury). He was also significant as one of the noblemen who pressured King John into signing the Magna Carta. There was a rival scheme by a French scholar called Hugo de Sancto Caro, but it was Stephen Langton's version that stuck.

The French, though, can claim the invention of Bible verses as one of theirs. It happened 300 years later. The man responsible was a publisher and academic called Robert Estiennes. He printed a huge number of books in his lifetime, and one was a version of the Bible with an accompanying volume that allowed people to find where various words occur in the Bible. (Books like this are still published today. They are called concordances.) He divided the chapters into verses so that it was easier to track down significant words.

His son Henri finished the task at the end of the sixteenth century after he inherited the business. He explained that the bulk of the work was done by his father in 1551 during a horseback journey from Paris to Lyons. (Presumably he worked on it during overnight stops. It's hard enough to study the Bible on the 119 bus to Croydon, let alone on a horse.)

Thanks to all these people, the Bible is ready for you to uncover. Sometimes you will find it called by different names. Very often the title on the cover is The Holy Bible. 'Holy' means set apart, and is an indication that Christians regard it as extremely special. Occasionally it is referred to as the Christian Scriptures. 'Scripture' means a collection of writings. And there are many variations available because it's translated from a foreign language. Lots of people have had a go at creating a version in their own language as time has gone by. All of them are good in their own way, and will certainly repay the time you put into them.

That leaves one obvious question before you start reading what has become the world's bestseller. What does 'Bible' mean? It means 'the book'. Simple as that!

During the coronation of Queen Elizabeth II, the Archbishop of Canterbury presented her with a Bible. The words he said were, 'We present you with this book, the most valuable thing that this world affords. Here is wisdom. This is the royal law. These are the lively oracles of God.' Scintillating words! Was he overselling it? There's only one way to find out.

BARE NECESSITIES!

Each chapter of this book ends with three ways to start uncovering the Bible. They involve increasing levels of commitment. The first is an extract that takes only a couple of minutes to read and is reproduced here to make this effortless. The second requires you to find a Bible and track down a longer passage. The third guides you through a substantial part of the Bible and will take the best part of an evening. Take your pick!

The first book of the New Testament is a biography of Jesus. It's called the Gospel of Matthew. Gospel means 'the good news'. Matthew is probably the name of the writer, but it's anyone's guess who he actually was. One of Jesus' 12 closest associates was called Matthew so it's tempting to hope it might have been him, but it was a common name and there's no reason why it should have been.

After some introductory information, Matthew starts to tell you about Jesus' life and teaching, and he quotes Jesus as saying these phenomenal words:

> 'You have heard that it was said, "Love your neighbour and hate your enemy." But I tell you, love your enemies and pray for those who persecute you, that you may be children of your Father in heaven. He causes his sun to rise on the evil and the good, and sends rain on the righteous and the unrighteous. If you love those who love you, what reward will you get? Are not even the tax collectors doing that? And if you greet only your own people, what are you doing more than others? Do not even pagans do that? Be perfect, therefore, as your heavenly Father is perfect.
>
> 'Be careful not to do your "acts of righteousness" before others, to be seen by them. If you do, you will have no reward from your Father in heaven. So when you give to the needy, do not announce it with trumpets, as the hypocrites do in the synagogues and on the streets, to be honoured by others. I tell you the truth, they have received their reward in full. But when you give to the needy, do not let your left hand know what your right hand is doing, so that your giving may be in secret. Then your Father, who sees what is done in secret, will reward you.'

Each time you see this symbol, there is an opportunity to pause and think about how words from the Bible might influence your own life. This time, there are some questions for you.

The saying about loving your enemies has become famous. Do you think Jesus meant what he said as a realistic way of handling relationships or as a memorable exaggeration? Would it work? How would it change the way you treat the neighbours from hell?

Does anything about sounding a trumpet fanfare when you give to the needy remind you of ways people donate to charity today? Might Jesus have a point?

BARELY MORE!

To get a sense of what it's like to start reading the Bible, read Matthew 1—7 (in other words, the first seven chapters of the Gospel of Matthew). It will take about half an hour, which is the same as an episode of *EastEnders*. Think of it as Middle EastEnders! You will find the words of Jesus you've just read towards the end (Matthew chapter 5, verse 43, to chapter 6, verse 4).

You may find that the words in your Bible are slightly different from the ones printed above, but the meaning will be the same. The English translation from which I quoted Jesus' words is called the New International Version, but there are several others and it doesn't matter which one you read. My advice would be to choose one that has been translated during the last 50 years rather than one with antiquated language.

Matthew begins with a family tree of Jesus' ancestors, going all the way back to a man called Abraham. You can skip that, but if you do read it, you might recognize some of the names because Matthew wanted readers to think that every celebrity in the history of the Jews was somehow related to Jesus.

After that comes the story of Jesus' birth. If you have ever seen a primary school nativity play, you will realize that some of the well-known elements are missing. Mary, Joseph, the angel and the wise men are there, but there are no shepherds, no donkey and nobody turns Mary and Joseph away from the inn at Bethlehem.

Of the four Gospels, two of them recount how Jesus came to be born. This is Matthew's version, and Luke includes the story of the shepherds visiting Jesus as a baby. People reading the Bible for the first time are taken by surprise that the most well-known story in it does not appear in every biography of Jesus. Does this pose a problem to scholars when they are trying to establish its historical accuracy? To be honest, yes! But it's not an impossible problem, as you will find out later in this book.

The next part of Matthew's Gospel is a subplot. Thirty years have passed. Matthew starts to tell the story of Jesus' cousin John, who was important because he was the first to recognize the mature Jesus for who he was.

Then the account of what Jesus said and did as an adult gets underway. Temptations are overcome and sermons are preached. Jesus gathers around him 12 men who are going to be his confidants and helpers over the next three years. Healings take place, bringing him to the attention of a large number of people.

Matthew then writes a long passage about the teaching Jesus gave. Traditionally this has been known as the Sermon on the Mount. However, it feels more as though the author has researched talks that Jesus gave at different times during his career and edited extracts together.

There are statements about the people who are blessed by God. They are full of surprises and defy usual expectations. There are demands about how we should live together as families and communities. There's help to know how to pray to God. There is a beautiful passage about how putting your trust in God can help you deal with everyday worries. And there are life-affirming assertions about the richness that being a follower of Jesus can bring to a person's life. Here's something to think about as you investigate Jesus' teaching.

The crowds flocking to Jesus at this point were needy – people with sick relatives, poor farmers and fishermen, men and women who had been conquered by an oppressive enemy. What would they have made of these words the first time they were uttered by Jesus? Does anything seem impossible to relate to our very different culture in the twenty-first century?

UNCOVERED!

Read the whole of Mark's Gospel. It's the shortest of the four biographies and takes about two hours to read. That's some way short of the men's marathon world record, you don't have to go into training and I've factored in time to make a coffee halfway through.

It was the first of the Gospels to be written. That was in about 66, just over 30 years after the events it describes and during the lifetime of eyewitnesses. It's full of fast-moving action with

Jesus portrayed as unique, outspoken and remarkable. It contains the whole unbearably tragic arc of Jesus' life and murder. And it ends with the first hint of Christian hope that God can overcome death itself.

2 Enjoying the Bible

The reason Christians treasure the Bible is not just because they enjoy it, but because they use it. In every part of the world in which it is read, and through all the centuries of its existence, Christians have had a profound sense that when they read the Bible God is communicating with them.

And that's where the problems begin!

The Bible is not a book that will tell you what to do. It will inspire you, guide you and inform you, but it will not tell you what to do. At least, not in the sense that a book of recipes gives you instructions that you follow in the hope of achieving something as perfect as the photograph. Working out what God wants you to do as a result of reading the Bible takes practice, because it isn't always obvious.

If you are lucky, the first time you open a Bible there will be a direction from God that speaks straight to your heart. It might be challenging to put it into practice, but it leaves you in no doubt as to what you are supposed to do. Here is an extract from the Bible that is just like that and it comes from the First Letter of John chapter 4, verses 7 and 12. (I'm going to quit spelling it out from now on and use the traditional method for referencing Bible passages. It's 1 John 4.7, 12.)

> Dear friends, let us love one another, for love comes from God . . . No one has ever seen God; but if we love one another, God lives in us and his love is made complete in us.

This message is the beating heart of the Christian faith. It's not straightforward – because the concept of the invisible God being within us is mysterious as well as magnificent – but it tells the followers of Jesus what they should do. They don't just tolerate one other; they love one other.

Just do what the Bible says and you'll be a fine Christian . . . unless you strike it unlucky the first time you try reading it. This is from Deuteronomy 23.12–14 (and it's the point where anyone who invested in a book called *The Bare Bible* hoping for a work of high literary merit will be dismayed to find that we sink to the bottom quite early on):

> Designate a place outside the camp where you can go to relieve yourself. As part of your equipment have something to dig with, and when you relieve yourself, dig a hole and cover up your excrement. For the Lord your God moves about in your camp to protect you and to deliver your enemies to you. Your camp must be holy, so that he will not see among you anything indecent and turn away from you.

Just doing what the Bible tells you to do really is not going to work. You can be a faithful, obedient Christian and still have a flushable toilet.

People react to this in different ways. It's not unusual for Christians to be told that they pick and choose which parts of the Bible they want to obey. This chapter of Deuteronomy illustrates the predicament all by itself. It includes a command that if a slave runs away you should give her refuge and not hand her back to the owner. (We like this.) It explains how a man who is irritated by his wife can divorce her simply by signing a certificate. (We don't like this.) And it has instructions for what a man should do if he has a wet dream. (We . . . actually, I've no idea what to think about that.)

I am hoping that this book can help you find a more satisfying way of reading the Bible than picking and choosing. This starts by realizing that it is not a book of instructions. It's a library of biographies, stories, poems, visions and letters. And all of it is the Bible. Every single scrap. All of it was originally included for a purpose, and can influence the way you think and the way you live. Even the poo-stick chapter, with its strange threat that God might abandon you if he sees you answering the call of nature. We'll come back to that. I hope it will make more sense by the end of this chapter.

In order to make the most of the Bible you need to ask yourself two questions. First, what did these words I'm reading mean to the people who first heard them? Second, if that is what the impact was on the first readers 20 centuries or more ago, what would God say to the world or to me individually to have the same impact today?

I'm going to come back to this two-stage process repeatedly, so I ought to introduce a couple of technical words. You can happily forget them, because they will never come up in everyday conversation, but don't forget what they mean. The two of them combined turn the Bible from a work of marvellous literature gleaming in history into a book through which God can make himself known to you.

The first word is *exegesis*. It means studying the Bible to work out its original context and the intentions of those who wrote it. The second word is *hermeneutics*. It means interpreting what you have discovered through exegesis so that it conveys meaning to our completely changed culture hundreds of years later.

You cannot do hermeneutics without first doing exegesis. To put it in a more forthright way, you can't take a sentence from the Bible and slap it across the twenty-first century as if nothing whatever had changed in the intervening years.

The men and women who wrote the Bible believed that the sun rotated around the earth. (That's probably what Jesus thought, but there's no way of knowing.) We are now sure beyond any possible doubt that they were mistaken, but the former belief accounts for songs of praise like this, which is part of Psalm 19.1–6:

> The heavens declare the glory of God;
> the skies proclaim the work of his hands . . .
> In the heavens God has pitched a tent for the sun,
> which is like a bridegroom coming forth from his pavilion,
> like a champion rejoicing to run his course.
> It rises at one end of the heavens
> and makes its circuit to the other;
> nothing is hidden from its heat.

If you do hermeneutics without doing exegesis (in other words, interpret it without really understanding it), you might assume that the only way you can accept the Bible is to reject the astronomy of the last six centuries and demand the Bible's view of the world is the correct one. If you do exegesis first, however, you realize that the poet was doing his absolute best with the scientific information that was available to him at the time. When he looked at the science, it caused him to marvel at the glory of the God, sustaining the world day after day after day. If you go on to interpret this for today (in other words, do hermeneutics), you realize that astronomy has shown the cosmos to be bigger, older, more complex and more wondrous than the poet could have imagined. Does that diminish a believer's sense of the glory of God? Absolutely the opposite!

One of the reasons this might seem controversial is that the beginning of the Bible describes a world created by God in six days, not brought into existence by God through a process of evolution over 13 billion years.

There are two groups of people who think you need to choose between those world views. One is a group of Christians who reject mainstream science and propose an alternative explanation of how the world came to be. Their world view treats the first page of the Bible as a textbook of geology and biology. (This way of thinking is called fundamentalism.) The other is a group of people who reject the Bible in its entirety (and perhaps any notion of God). They do so because what they have read in the Old Testament strikes them as irrelevant to a world in which we now know there are 200 billion suns like ours in the Milky Way galaxy alone.

The reason I've written *The Bare Bible* is that you don't have to belong to either of those groups. With a bit of help you can both understand why this ancient library says what it says *and* discover that it has a life-enhancing impact on you in this decade. And since you have proved yourself willing to tolerate the intellectual demands of exegesis and hermeneutics, let's leave the lecture room and head back to the toilet!

Why does the Bible give obsolete instructions about how to deal with our waste? The book of rules for those who worshipped God was written many centuries before Jesus. (We'll investigate how many in a later chapter.) The men of God who formulated these laws knew a bit of rudimentary science and medicine. Bacteria and their related diseases were not identified until the seventeenth century, but in ancient times learned men had observed that where human and animal waste was allowed to infect food, illness followed. So, many of the rules of the Old Testament were imposed in order to improve the health of the community. For instance, there were commands that forbade foods likely to cause sickness and instructed men and women how to deal with mould. God longed for his people, among whom he was a real but invisible presence, to live in a place of health, decency and protection.

If you look behind an apparently obscure reference in the Bible and ask why it was written there thousands of years ago, it's then possible to work out what is important to God. (That's working out the context – exegesis.) The well-being of humankind is something that is as vital to him now as it was then. This principle finds its equivalent today in Christian development charities that work among the poorest communities in the world to ensure that wells provide clean water, sanitation is available and families have soap. And it drove the Christian philanthropists of the Victorian era to build housing in British cities that had adequate sanitation and sewerage. (That's working out the implications for today – hermeneutics.) God's love is as practical as it is spiritual, which means that every sign that says 'Now wash your hands' is in an Old Testament tradition.

Bacteria have no religious views, so Christians promoting hygiene then and now don't just seek the health of other Christians, but of all people. The concept of a kingdom in which health, peace and justice are a constant reality for people under God's rule is an essential theme that threads through the Bible, as we shall see.

Most of us need help to do exegesis, and that is why there is a history of thorough academic study of the Bible. It's called theology. Indeed, everyone who thinks about God and life is a theologian, including you at this moment, but some people make it a lifetime's work, which is a great help to anyone who wants to read the Bible in an intelligent way. Their expertise reveals things that are not immediately obvious to people reading the Bible for the first time. They put the words we are reading into the context of the world their writers lived in – its politics, its culture and the nature of the other literature of the time.

Academics can tell us about subtleties of the meaning of words in their original languages. They research the dates and the places in which the books were originally written. They find out what archaeology and history can uncover about places that are mentioned in the Bible. They think about what might have happened to the stories and sayings before they came to be written down, as they were passed from generation to generation by word of mouth. And they try to work out why the writers chose to shape and select the material they had got, leaving out some incidents and including others.

The books that scholars write about the Bible are called commentaries. Sometimes they examine the Bible sentence by sentence, or even word by word. Of course, all theologians bring their own assumptions to their study and it's not unusual for them to disagree with each other.

Here's an example. The first written record of the life of Jesus that we have in the Bible was made about 30 years after his death and resurrection. Academics are very interested in what happened to the accounts of what he said and did during those three decades. Some think that Jesus' words were so significant to his followers that they were memorized with great precision and reproduced in the New Testament that Christians now read. Others think that the records we have of Jesus' words were given a particular emphasis because church leaders at the time they were written down, later in the first century, needed to encourage their congregations in the light of what was going on around them.

For instance, at the time when the stories of Jesus were being written down, terrible suffering had overtaken Jerusalem. The words of Jesus about the appalling distress his followers would undergo were extremely accurate. There are two ways of looking at that: either Jesus had a God-given foresight into what would happen to the city, or the Bible writers shaped his words in such a way that those who were living through dreadful anguish would find hope.

All of us can make up our own minds. Most people don't have to tell anyone what they've decided, but if you are a professor of theology, writing a book, you do. You might take a conservative view and write your book assuming that we have very accurate records of Jesus' words and of Jewish history. You might take a liberal view and assume that the Bible writers created a version of history that suited what their original readers needed.

You will want to know which of the alternatives *The Bare Bible* opts for. Neither! What I am keen to do in this book is to persuade you to read this absorbing but complicated library. I will try to give all the different points of view. You can decide what you make of it.

The reason I hope you will start reading the Bible is that people without any special training at all find it seizes their imagination. It can become one of the ways through which God guides individuals and nations. If you read it thinking you're going to find magical messages from God addressed personally to you, either disillusion or disaster will follow, but Christians who use both exegesis and hermeneutics say confidently that there is a sense in which the Bible directs them.

People who allow it to have some kind of authority over their thoughts and their way of life find that it isn't a dry academic study, but a way of filling their days with meaning, goodness and hope. There are insights in it that chime so perfectly with your experience of life that they seem to lay your soul bare. There are also parts that are very disturbing, and I promise that this book won't duck out of those. The overarching message that comes from reading the Bible, however, is that human life has a purpose because there is a good and loving God.

That's exhilarating. It's worth battling with the apparent contradictions and complexity. The Bible is reliable, but it's not infallible. It's not scientifically accurate in the way we would expect a textbook to be today because it doesn't speak the language of quantum mechanics; it speaks the language of faith.

This is how the Bible describes itself – literature that is inspired by God but communicated through ordinary men and women writing in a particular place and era. It comes in 2 Peter 1.21. Exegesis would reveal that it was originally written just about the Old Testament. Hermeneutics suggests to me that it is equally true of the Bible as a whole: 'Prophets, though human, spoke from God as they were carried along by the Holy Spirit.'

BARE NECESSITIES!

I'm pretty sure that if you've never read it before, this story from the life of Jesus is going to unsettle you. Just read it and see what you make of it. It comes from Mark 5.1–20:

> They went across the lake to the region of the Gerasenes. When Jesus got out of the boat, a man with an evil spirit came from the tombs to meet him. This man lived in the tombs, and no one could bind him anymore, not even with a chain. For he had often been chained hand and foot, but he tore the chains apart and broke the irons on his feet. No one was strong enough to subdue him. Night and day among the tombs and in the hills he would cry out and cut himself with stones. When he saw Jesus from a distance, he ran and fell on his knees in front of him. He shouted at the top of his voice, 'What do you want with me, Jesus, Son of the Most High God? Swear to God that you won't torture me!' For Jesus had said to him, 'Come out of this man, you evil spirit!'
>
> Then Jesus asked him, 'What is your name?'
>
> 'My name is Legion,' he replied, 'for we are many.' And he begged Jesus again and again not to send them out of the area.
>
> A large herd of pigs was feeding on the nearby hillside. The demons begged Jesus, 'Send us among the pigs; allow us to go into them.' He gave them permission, and the impure spirits came out and went into the pigs. The herd, about two thousand in number, rushed down the steep bank into the lake and were drowned.

Those tending the pigs ran off and reported this in the town and countryside, and the people went out to see what had happened. When they came to Jesus, they saw the man who had been possessed by the legion of demons, sitting there, dressed and in his right mind; and they were afraid. Those who had seen it told the people what had happened to the demon-possessed man – and told about the pigs as well. Then the people began to plead with Jesus to leave their region.

As Jesus was getting into the boat, the man who had been demon-possessed begged to go with him. Jesus did not let him, but said, 'Go home to your family and tell them how much the Lord has done for you, and how he has had mercy on you.' So the man went away and began to tell in the Decapolis how much Jesus had done for him. And all the people were amazed.

I know what you're thinking. Those poor pigs! How could Jesus be so cruel?

We need to do some exegesis.

Jesus was Jewish and he lived in the first century in the lands now shared by Israel and Palestine. Life for a Jew at that time was utterly wretched. Their lands were occupied by the army of the vast and totalitarian Roman Empire. They were treated brutally, they lived in fear, and they loathed paying taxes to a government they regarded as an enemy.

Now, I expect you've got friends who are Jewish. If you invited them for a meal, what is the one thing you would never serve them? You've got it!

The Jews hated pigs with all their might. They had been commanded for centuries not to eat them or even go near them.

They were vermin. We think the same way about rats. So why were they there? Because the Romans absolutely loved their bacon. They were aggressively farming pigs in the land they had conquered despite the fact that it totally revolted the Jews.

So when Jesus drove out pigs, he was getting rid of vermin. He was also giving a sweeping political gesture of what was going to happen to the Roman oppressors when God took control. Every evil thing they did would be swept away. This was an area where many Roman soldiers lived – no wonder they wanted Jesus to leave.

I don't suppose the poor soul who called himself Legion was possessed by evil. I imagine he had a severe mental illness, but the best medics of the day described that as demon possession. You can't really blame Mark for describing it as he did. He was doing his best with the information he had, but he didn't have superhuman knowledge of what psychiatrists would discover (and are still discovering) 20 centuries later. There is something wondrous, though, about the fact that, in the presence of Jesus, the man found calm.

Has this information, which puts the story in context, changed the way you think about it in any way?

BARELY MORE!

To discover some more about the life of Jesus, read Luke 4.14—6.16. Here are some facts that are not immediately clear from what you read, but that may help you grasp its significance more fully.

The sermon that Jesus gave in Nazareth is usually thought of as the beginning of Jesus' mission. The issue that drove the men to violence against him was that the examples he chose of people in the Old Testament on whom God lavished love were foreigners. Jesus was telling a Jewish crowd that God's love extended to everyone in the world, not just Jews.

So yes, Jesus' mission really did begin with a brawl. It's up to you how vigorously you imagine Jesus 'walked right through the crowd' when they tried to kill him, but I don't suppose it was pretty.

The people to whom Jesus shows kindness in these stories is also significant. People with leprosy were wrongly thought to be such a danger to the community that they were outcasts. Touching a person who had leprosy would be thought of as disgusting by the Jews of Jesus' time. Tax collectors were also despised, but not for the reason you might think! The Jews loathed paying taxes to their conquerors, but some decided to take highly paid jobs collecting tax on behalf of the Roman Empire. They were collaborating with the enemy, so you can imagine how friendless they became.

Pharisees were ultra-religious Jews. They demanded obedience to so many rules that all the humanity had been squeezed out of them. Jesus detested their ways, as you'll see in the next chapter of this book. You would think that relieving someone's misery by healing them was a wonderful thing, but it counted as work if you were a Pharisee. So, if you did it on the Jewish day of rest, the Sabbath, you'd broken God's law. (Yes, I know – ridiculous!) Guess which day Jesus chose to heal a man with atrophied muscles in his hand. Yup!

You now have some head knowledge about those chapters. Do they say anything to your heart?

UNCOVERED!

If you have half an hour to spare, keep reading Luke until the end of chapter 13. You will encounter miracles, stories with a meaning (called parables – Jesus often used them in his teaching), and a man of extraordinary compassion. See whether Jesus inspires you. The next two chapters of this book are all about him.

3 The biographies of Jesus

There are four accounts of Jesus' life in the Bible. They begin the New Testament, and they are known as Gospels. They are presumably named after the authors – Matthew, Mark, Luke and John.

Nothing very substantial was written about Jesus during the 30 years after his life. The stories were kept vividly alive, told and retold as increasing numbers of people started to worship him as their God. But although Jesus was an intellectual, he had surrounded himself with people who were mostly illiterate – fishermen, for instance, or women whose opportunity for education was very limited. On the last occasion they met, Jesus promised his followers that he would return in triumph, so there was initially an expectation that it would happen any day. It didn't occur to the first Christians that 2,000 years on there would still be people with a huge appetite to know what happened. The return of which Jesus spoke has taken longer than anyone imagined. Children were being born who needed to be told about the events that had transformed their parents' world. The eyewitnesses who had the most accurate memories were coming to the ends of their lives. It became vital to get a written record before the stories either lost their detail or became exaggerated.

People who study these things have come to the conclusion that Mark's was the first Gospel to be written. He emphasizes Jesus' warning to his followers that terrible things might happen to them because they follow him, but that it would be a way of life they never regretted. It seems evident that something dreadful was happening to Christians while Mark was writing, so theologians guess that it was during the period when the Roman Emperor Nero was demanding that Christians either curse Jesus or face death. (He had them dipped in tar and burnt alive to illuminate the gardens of his palace. I already wish I hadn't told you that.) Give or take a couple of years, 66 is a good guess as to when Mark was written.

About 300 years later a historian wrote that Mark talked to Jesus' close friend Peter, who was the source of the stories. That's a nice thought, but nobody takes it very seriously. What seems more likely is that collections of Jesus' sayings were being passed around and Mark built a biography from them, speaking to as many eyewitnesses as he could find. His account races through Jesus' life from the age of 30 onwards, filling it with action and highly political outbursts that would have been full of meaning for people suffering at the hands of a tyrannical regime.

About ten years later Matthew wrote his Gospel. There is one date we can be sure about, which is that Jerusalem and the Jewish Temple were destroyed by the Roman army after a siege in 70. Some parts of Matthew refer to this event in such detail that they could only have been written after it, which is how theologians deduce the date. It is also clear that Matthew possessed a copy of Mark's Gospel, because he plagiarized chunks of it word for word. He also had new information to add from his own research and other sources – particularly about Jesus' birth and the extraordinary events that followed his death. He was very keen to explain how events in Jesus' life fulfilled things that had been anticipated by the Old Testament centuries before. This leads people to conclude that he was writing for Jewish readers, who would have known the Old Testament well because it was their holiest book. Mark may have been writing for non-Jews (the technical word is 'Gentiles') because whenever he uses a Jewish term he explains it, whereas Matthew doesn't bother.

Over the next 100 years dozens of accounts of Jesus' life were composed. Many of the stories of Jesus were dismissed by Christian leaders a century later as over-sensational. The four Gospels we have in the Bible were chosen as part of a rigorous process of selection because they were seen as reliable.

The Gospel of Luke seems to have been commissioned specifically so that among the junk there would be a dependable, thoroughly researched account. The prologue names a man called Theophilus for whom Luke wrote. (It means 'lover of God', so it may simply be that Luke was writing for everyone who loves God in order to explain why the life of Jesus had transformed the world.)

Luke ripped off Mark's Gospel, just as Matthew did. There are some stories that appear in Matthew and Luke, but not Mark. They are so similar that scholars believe there was an anthology of sayings and stories about Jesus from which they both copied, but which hasn't survived. It's called Q (not so intriguing a title as it seems – it's short for the German word for 'source'). Luke also includes some stories that don't appear elsewhere, and seems very interested in the detail of occasions on which Jesus heals someone. (Might he have been a doctor? Elsewhere in the New Testament there is a Luke described as a doctor.) If the most obvious feature of Jesus in Mark is that he is full of action, the thing you notice most in Luke is that he is full of compassion. The three biographies are so similar that theologians call them the Synoptic Gospels – it means 'they see eye to eye'.

The fourth Gospel, named after John, is rather different. It isn't a comprehensive account of the life of Jesus. Instead it focuses on a few crucial events. It describes them at length, then gives a sort of commentary on them. It's a bit like what a preacher would do in a sermon, so that the significance of Jesus' actions in God's plan for humankind becomes clear. For instance, John tells the miraculous story of how Jesus healed a man with a long-standing disability. Accusations follow, which lead to Jesus declaring that everything he does has the authority of God and even greater, life-transforming signs that he is the Son of God are imminent. (The word 'sign' comes up a lot.)

Most people think John's Gospel was written at the end of the first century, and the writing certainly has the feel that many decades of reflection on what Jesus taught have gone into it. There is a tradition that the John who wrote it was someone described in the book as Jesus' best friend, but if that were the case he would have been the oldest man on the planet by the time he started writing. It's more likely that he inspired it, but the author is anonymous. Like Luke, he tells us why he wrote it. This comes almost at the end (John 20.30–31):

> Jesus did many other miraculous signs in the presence of his disciples, which are not recorded in this book. But these are written that you may believe that Jesus is the Christ, the Son of God, and that by believing you may have life in his name.

Hang on to the word 'Messiah'. It will help you understand a lot about the New Testament. It's a Hebrew word, and the biggest controversy surrounding Jesus during and after his lifetime was whether or not he could claim that title. You will grasp its significance much more clearly when I tell you what its equivalent is in the Greek language. It's 'Christ'. The name Jesus Christ is not a Christian name followed by a surname. Jesus was a fairly common name, but Jesus Christ was an audacious claim that this particular Jesus was and is the Messiah.

I expect you remember from the last chapter that Jesus was Jewish, and the lands in which the Jews of the first century lived had been conquered. They were now part of the vast Empire of Rome, and Tiberius Caesar ruled as a tyrant. It was a period of great misery and oppression for the Jews.

However, their Scriptures (our Old Testament) had led them to expect that God would send them a leader who would raise an army, overthrow their conquerors and establish a golden age of independence and prosperity. They called that leader the Messiah (it means 'the anointed one').

Now, does that sound like Jesus? Well, no!

The four Gospels explain how someone who refused to countenance violence, preached that love should so fill people's lives that it even extended to the Romans, and was executed aged 33 came to be regarded as the Messiah. They are the good news of Jesus the Christ.

Just after he turned 30, Jesus made a visit to his cousin John. John was the leader of a religious revival. He was living by the River Jordan, where he dressed up like a wild Old Testament hero and thundered out sermons about how the Messiah was on his way. He preached about the need for people to have a dramatic change in the integrity of their lifestyles if they were to be ready for what God was going to do. Crowds flocked to him and lapped it up.

John baptized Jesus in the river. (He is sometimes known as John the Baptist.) For Jesus it was a profound moment because he was overwhelmed with the immensity of God's love for him. He described it as being like a son and father. It was John who first recognized that Jesus was exceptional. Other young men had raised rebellious mobs, styled themselves Messiah, struck some blows, but come to sticky ends. John saw in Jesus something different altogether.

For a start, Jesus had been extremely well educated as a Jewish rabbi in his home town, Nazareth. People commented on how authoritative he was as a preacher. On one notable occasion he gave a sermon in his local synagogue about God's plan to bring poverty and oppression to an end. The congregation, weary of day-after-day cruelty, initially loved his message. However, Jesus went on to say that God's love was not going to liberate only the Jews but also the entire world. Every nation on earth was going to experience God's healing and forgiveness. His Jewish audience thought this was an outrage and they set on him. In the skirmish that followed he came close to losing his life.

He needed a new home, so he moved to Capernaum by Lake Galilee. He gathered around him a close-knit group of 12 men. They included a fisherman called Peter, who went on to become the leader of the first church, and Judas, whose actions three years later were to lead to Jesus' death.

They travelled widely through the villages around Galilee and occasionally visited Jerusalem, the capital city. Jesus gained a reputation as someone who could work miracles. His arrival in a village was greeted with excitement because there was an expectation that he could restore sick people to health. He described some of those healings as evil spirits being cast out by God's intervention. (You may remember that the last chapter explained how this was one of the ways mental illness was understood in that era.)

He made a point of befriending marginalized people. He was drawn towards poor people with a huge compassion. Women and children were treated with complete respect, which was unexpected in that culture. (In fact, a group of wealthy women who became his followers funded his mission.) He kept company with people whom others treated as outcasts.

His way was completely different from other Jewish leaders. He was repeatedly critical of their loveless demands that people should be religious. He really enjoyed a party, but would sometimes get so exhausted that he took himself off to secluded places to pray. He stayed single, which was unusual for a man of his status at that time. And, most importantly, he was loved.

The number of Jesus' followers grew. They are usually called disciples, meaning that they followed his way of life as well as following him literally. At the height of his popularity they numbered thousands. For three remarkable years broken people were healed, destitute people found hope, and Jewish men and women saw that an alternative to the injustice that overwhelmed them might be possible.

There was endless talk about whether Jesus was the Messiah, but whenever he was asked he evaded the question. He would say, 'Look at what's happening and work it out for yourselves.' There was also controversy about where Jesus' ability to perform miracles came from. People accused him of having done a deal with the devil in order to get magical powers, but Jesus said that the truth was precisely the opposite. The reason miracles were taking place was that God had begun to establish a brand new kingdom. In this kingdom, poverty, hunger, injustice and illness would be brought to an end once and for all. As you can imagine, the talk of a new kingdom did not go down well with those who felt their power was threatened. Jesus began to make influential enemies – both political and religious.

There was a long-standing expectation among the Jews that when the Messiah rose to overthrow the Roman army it would be at the time of an annual celebration called the Passover. It was a festival of freedom from oppression, the anniversary of a triumph centuries before. (You will discover more about it in Chapter 7.) At the start of the last week of his life, Jesus headed for Jerusalem to celebrate the festival there. His disciples, frightened but gripped, wondered whether this would be the moment when the uprising began. Some of them armed themselves, but Jesus had other ideas.

He entered Jerusalem riding a donkey, surrounded by pilgrims cheering and waving branches. They flung their cloaks in front of the procession, which Jews had done in ancient times to hail a king. They shouted acclamations from the Old Testament that were associated with the Messiah. At a time when tensions were already high, everything about this was provocative.

Jesus was parodying a man called Pontius Pilate, who was the Roman charged with governing Jerusalem. He was a sadist who had treated the Jews with cruelty and disdain for their religious rituals. Jesus was forcing the crowds to a decision. Would they tolerate being downtrodden by an emperor who ruled by fear from a thousand miles away? Or would they choose a kingdom in which the poor heard good news, the suffering were cared for and the oppressed were freed? But he wasn't doing it with violence; he was enjoying all the elation of a festival.

The crowd was mad for it but, unexpectedly, Jesus showed no heroics. Instead he wept for a place he loved in which there was no peace. Having set the Roman government on high alert, he immediately went on to challenge the Jewish high priests. He went to the Temple and preached his customary message that all people of all nations were entitled to pray to the God who loved them. In the courtyard were traders who operated a system under which only goods approved by the Temple authorities could be used in worship, sold with an extortionate mark-up. The impact of this on the poor made Jesus furious, and he hurled their merchandise and furniture around. Both the political and religious leaders were incensed, but it was difficult for them to know how to stop it because the crowds adored him.

Jesus marked the Passover, as all Jews did and still do, with a meal surrounded by his followers. However, there were two things about this Passover that were exceptional. One was that Jesus unsettled the other guests by performing the actions they would have expected from one of the servants. He washed their feet, muddy from the streets, and as he did so explained that in the kingdom of God leadership was a matter of serving people, not lording it over them.

The other drew attention to two of the traditional Passover foods. He thanked God for the bread and broke it (which was not unusual), but then added, 'This is my body, take it and eat it' (which was extraordinary). As he passed round the cup of wine, he told them that they were drinking his blood, which was going to be poured out so that the sins of the world would be forgiven.

His shed blood, he declared, was the new covenant that God was making. It was God's new way of relating to humankind; his new testament. He told his followers to eat bread and drink wine whenever they gathered so that he would always be remembered. This is something that, in many ways and under various names, Christians have always done in their churches.

It was during this meal that Judas, one of Jesus' followers, decided for reasons that have never been clear to organize his arrest. He left the room, went to the Jewish leaders, and let them know the best time and place to apprehend Jesus without a crowd there to protect him. He was paid 30 silver pieces for betraying his friend.

In a quiet garden called Gethsemane Jesus stopped to pray. He was in torment, because he knew suffering and death lay ahead, but he also recognized that, if he decided to submit to it, he was the central figure in a world-changing plan of God. Judas arrived and greeted Jesus with apparent affection. It was, though, a prearranged sign for soldiers to seize him. Jesus offered no resistance and his terrified friends fled.

Jesus faced two trials. The first was in front of the Jewish high court. The priests accused him of claiming to be the Messiah. When he stayed silent they sentenced him to death for blasphemy. They didn't have the authority to carry out the execution, though, so they sent him to Pontius Pilate, the Roman Governor. Pilate despised the Jewish authorities and was fascinated by Jesus, so he made an attempt to save him. Thinking it would win him the admiration of the crowds, he offered to set Jesus free. However, rabble-rousers who supported the Jewish leaders turned the mob against Jesus. Bound, beaten and covered with spit, he no longer looked like the Messiah they had hoped for a week before. They bayed for blood. Pilate washed his hands of the whole affair and signed Jesus' death warrant.

The soldiers subjected Jesus to a mock coronation, paraded him through the streets to Calvary, which was the city's execution site, stripped him naked and crucified him. In agony, Jesus shouted hymns from the Old Testament and, remarkably, prayed to God to forgive his murderers. After about six hours he died.

A Jewish leader called Joseph found the courage to go to Pilate and ask for the corpse to be released so that Jesus could be buried with dignity. Jesus' body was placed in a cave-like tomb and a boulder was rolled across the entrance. It was done at speed before sunset because, this being a Friday, the Jewish holy day (the Sabbath) was about to begin. Jesus' followers undoubtedly spent the Saturday in shock at the tragedy they had just witnessed, but the usual rituals that would accompany a burial could not take place until the Sabbath was over on the Sunday.

Some 40 hours after they had seen Jesus die, his remaining disciples were together, scared and bereft. A group of agitated women burst in on them. Their message, which the men dismissed at first as absurd, was that they had been to the tomb to embalm Jesus' body. They had found the boulder rolled away and the cave empty. They had seen Jesus, not dead as they had expected but alive.

The four accounts of Jesus' life differ slightly in the way they describe what happened next. Between them they describe the aftermath of an earth tremor, angels beside the tomb announcing that Jesus was alive, and Jesus' closest friends running to the site and confirming that what the women had described was true. Over the next six weeks there were appearances by Jesus to individuals and groups. They were not spectacular; in fact they happened in humdrum locations.

On one occasion a woman called Mary Magdalene was out of control with tears. A man approached whom she assumed to be a gardener, but she recognized it to be Jesus when he called her name. On another occasion the 11 remaining disciples (Judas had committed suicide) met with Jesus and ate a meal together. Others were joined by Jesus beside the sea as they pulled their fishing boats to shore, or as they took a journey out of Jerusalem to a nearby village.

All the descriptions struggle because they are trying to convey something unprecedented. The witnesses could touch the scars on Jesus' wrists where he had been nailed to a cross, so this was not a ghost or a vision. But Jesus could come and go at will, even in a locked room, so this was not merely a body that had come back to life. It was unlike anything before or since. The word that Christians use for this unique event is resurrection.

Although the appearances of Jesus to his followers were initially frightening, increasingly they found them to be joyful and full of hope. The final appearance took place on a hill outside Jerusalem. Jesus commissioned his followers to take his teaching worldwide, creating new disciples who would live by his principles. He told them that although he would not be visible to them in the future, they would have an absolutely authentic sense of his presence with them wherever they went for as long as they lived. It would be a spiritual presence – his Holy Spirit. And one day, in triumph and quite unlike the way they had known him over recent years, he would return.

People who are uncovering the Bible for the first time will be asking, of course, whether these accounts of Jesus' life are reliable. It's an entirely reasonable question to ask.

The first thing to say is that, no matter what rumours you may have heard, there is no doubt whatever that Jesus existed. There is more evidence for his life than any other figure in ancient history. And not all the evidence comes from a Christian perspective – there are also references to Jesus by historians of the time who did not share the faith of the Gospel writers.

This book would not be doing its job, though, if I made out that there are no questions to be asked about whether everything in the accounts happened precisely as it is presented to us by the biographers. In fact, it isn't even really right to call the Gospels biographies, because the writers were not trying to present Jesus' life in its entirety. They were selective in the events about which they wrote. They edited the material they had so that they could put side by side things that didn't actually happen that way. You can tell this simply by comparing the four, because you quickly notice things happening in a different order or at a different location.

Sometimes the point that the writer is trying to make by putting stories together is so obvious that you grin at the lack of subtlety. For instance, at the very midpoint of his Gospel, Mark tells the story of Jesus healing a bind man. It's immediately fol-lowed by Jesus' followers having an eye-opening realization that Jesus is the Messiah. Coincidence? I think not!

If you are reading the story of Jesus for the first time it's helpful to remember that the Gospel writers were also influenced by the place and the time in which they were writing. The inci-dents from Jesus' life that they chose to write about were selected because they spoke directly to their first audience.

If the biographies were being written in the twenty-first century, they would undoubtedly have been more curious about romance. It's reasonable to assume that Jesus' teenage heart went a-flutter from time to time – he was human after all. So why is there nothing whatever about Jesus' adolescence? Because when Christians were reading the Gospels for the first time, their friends were being thrown to the lions, so it's hard to imagine that anyone cared. Instead, there are sober passages about suffering, and it is clear that the writers framed Jesus' words in such a way that they provided both warning and hope to the generation who first read them in the first century.

There is also a more debatable question of what happened to the stories about Jesus as they got told and retold during the decades between the events and the first written record. Some theologians suggest that we should assume that as believers told friends, who then told their families and neighbours, the stories must have lost some of their mundane details and picked up more intriguing ones. It's fair enough! The Gospel writers didn't have their words dictated by God through a UHF in-ear monitor. Rather, they prayerfully and with great dedication opened themselves to the Holy Spirit of God. They tried to get it right, but there was no Bluetooth in the first century.

There are places where Jesus is recorded as saying things that had an uncanny insight into his own future. He made it clear that he expected to be killed. However, he insisted that this was not a revolutionary's tragic end, but would be followed by resurrection. He spoke of his death as if it was the most important thing in his life. It was the climax of God's plan, and through it the entire world would be saved. Some theologians are inclined to see this as the Gospel writers using the benefit of hindsight.

Other theologians point out that Jesus was utterly unique. Here is a quote from a letter by one of the first Christian leaders

(Colossians 1.19): 'God was pleased to have all his fullness dwell in him.' That would mean there was nothing surprising whatever about Jesus knowing God's plan for his future. Theologians suggest that the teaching of Jesus was regarded as so important during those early years that there was an extreme effort to keep its precision. So it's likely that specific words and phrases were committed to memory or even written down and copied by those who were able to do so. That would mean we are able to read the sayings of Jesus and imagine his actual voice with confidence in their accuracy.

To be fair to those uncovering the Bible for the first time, I should add that there is a particular concern among some readers about the narratives that relate to Jesus' birth and those that describe appearances after his resurrection. The stories about Jesus' birth give historians a problem because we know from other sources the dates when particular events happened – for instance, the reigns of various rulers. No one seems to be able to make the stories that are told in Luke and Matthew fit conclusively.

Some people find it possible to imagine the writers researching the Old Testament for insights into what was expected when the Messiah came, and using what they found there to embellish their descriptions of Jesus' birth. They are certainly crammed with meaning. They reference Bethlehem, the birthplace of David, who was the greatest king in Israel's history. They speak of a baby conceived by a miraculous act of God, whose name would be Jesus (it means 'God will save us'). Matthew's version indicates that this salvation will have no national boundaries, because the young Jesus is visited by foreign intellectuals ('wise men'). Luke, taking the side of marginalized people from the start, records Jesus being visited by riff-raff (shepherds, guided there by angels).

The whole is overshadowed by tragedy, because Herod the Great (whom the Romans had installed as a so-called 'King of the Jews') heard rumours of a rival and had boy children massacred – a fate from which the infant Jesus escaped.

Every single syllable of these stories is heavy with religious significance. Primary school nativities relocate them everywhere from urban bus shelters to outer space. So it's entirely sensible to listen to commentators who feel that the reason for their inclusion in the Gospels is more to do with their meaning than their historical accuracy. But while you are nodding wisely at the intelligence of the theologians, don't forget that you also have permission to assume that these stories are in the Bible because that's what actually happened.

The difficulty presented by the stories of Jesus appearing to people after his resurrection is that the versions in the four Gospels describe them in different ways and, with the best will in the world, can't all be right. They have much in common, but they have contradictions too. For many readers it's sufficient that the writers would have spoken to eyewitnesses, each of whom would have had individual viewpoints and different recollections. It has even been suggested that the fact that there are variations means we should be more inclined to trust that Jesus rose from the dead, because it shows that his followers did not concoct a story and stick to it come what may.

Other readers have their doubts. They point out that Matthew is disarmingly honest in the closing sentences of his Gospel and writes that even the eyewitnesses to whom he spoke had their doubts as well.

We all have the same evidence. We all make up our minds.

What seems beyond dispute is that when the first Easter Sunday dawned, a group of astonished and frightened women found that the stone in front of Jesus' tomb had been rolled away and the body was gone. Within days, or perhaps even within hours, the entire community of Jesus' followers had become convinced that Jesus was alive. It is no exaggeration to say that it is solely because of that conviction that the Bible is being read worldwide 2,000 years later. Without it there would be hardly any interest in the life of Jesus. I would certainly not have written *The Bare Bible*. I would probably have written *The Plain Plato*.

The declaration that has driven people for 20 centuries to investigate the Bible, and that makes your decision to read it now a wise one, is this. Christians believe that in the middle of one night, in the pitch black of a cave, with absolutely no observers and needing no help from anyone, Jesus got on with what only God can do and silently came back from the dead.

BARE NECESSITIES!

This story is told in John 8.1–11. In it prominent Jewish figures in Jerusalem attempt to put Jesus in an impossible position, hoping for an opportunity to denounce him. I've chosen it because it shows Jesus as extremely clever as well as deeply compassionate. It also has a bit of a mystery – what did Jesus doodle in the dust?

> Jesus went to the Mount of Olives. At dawn he appeared again in the temple courts, where all the people gathered around him, and he sat down to teach them. The teachers of the law and the Pharisees brought in a woman caught in adultery. They made her stand before the group and said to

> Jesus, 'Teacher, this woman was caught in the act of adultery. In the Law Moses commanded us to stone such women. Now what do you say?' They were using this question as a trap, in order to have a basis for accusing him.
>
> But Jesus bent down and started to write on the ground with his finger. When they kept on questioning him, he straightened up and said to them, 'Let any one of you who is without sin be the first to throw a stone at her.' Again he stooped down and wrote on the ground.
>
> At this, those who heard began to go away one at a time, the older ones first, until only Jesus was left, with the woman still standing there. Jesus straightened up and asked her, 'Woman, where are they? Has no one condemned you?'
>
> 'No one, sir,' she said.
>
> 'Then neither do I condemn you,' Jesus declared. 'Go now and leave your life of sin.'

The Pharisees were extremely devout Jews. They were devoted admirably to obeying every detail of the Law, which had guided Jewish life for many centuries. (These rules are recorded in the Old Testament, and Chapter 8 of this book is about them.) They were attempting to create an exhaustive interpretation of the rules so that at any moment in the daily life of a Jewish person, he or she would know precisely what to do. It was so legalistic that people's humanity got crushed under its weight.

Jesus loathed it. He hated the fact that when there was a choice between rules and compassion, the rules won every time. He was an outspoken critic, which made him very unpopular with the Pharisees. Here they had a chance to discredit Jesus. They demanded to know which side he was going to take – the Jewish religion to which Jesus said he was utterly committed, or a terrified, vulnerable woman. They planned that whichever he chose, Jesus would lose face.

So then, who do you think won and who lost? Or is that not such a straightforward question?

BARELY MORE!

For a reasonably short read that gives a sense of both the thrill and the tension of all that happened during the final week of Jesus' life, I suggest John 12.1—14.8.

We pick up the story after one of the most remarkable events ascribed to Jesus. His friend Lazarus has died and, as is the custom in Middle Eastern countries, been placed speedily in a tomb. Jesus, heartbroken, demands that the rock sealing the entrance to the tomb is dragged away. Lazarus crawls out, having been restored to life by Jesus.

Chapter 12 begins in Lazarus' house with an unsettlingly intimate account of Jesus being caressed by one of his female followers. Then a crowd of people, still in awe of what happened to Lazarus, hold a rally for Jesus in which Bible verses associated with the Messiah are shouted. This further aggravates the Pharisees. Jesus, increasingly using the name 'Father' for God in order to show their closeness, anticipates that his death is imminent.

Jesus eats a final meal with his followers. To their astonishment, he waves away the servants who would be expected to wash them as they prepared to eat and takes the servant's role himself. He insists that this is a model of how his followers should relate to others. They should see themselves as servants to the world, not masters of it. This is a complete contrast to the expectations of the crowd who anticipated a Messiah who would conquer and rule. Understandably upset by talk of death, Jesus' disciples protest, so Jesus talks of God, of trust and of heaven.

The author of John's Gospel was writing about 70 years after these events. There had been plenty of time to reflect on the significance of events in Jesus' life. He must have chosen this selection for a reason. What conclusions do you think he wanted his readers to come to about Jesus?

UNCOVERED!

Keep reading for another hour to the end of John's Gospel. That's the same length as a *Game of Thrones* episode. Take in the whole horrendous tragedy of the end of Jesus' life, and then the account of his resurrection upon which the entirety of the Christian hope is founded.

4 The teaching of Jesus

Considering the fact that the four Gospels were written for different audiences over the course of four decades, the way they describe what Jesus taught his followers is very consistent. It has the ring of truth, but the ways the writers present that teaching are very different.

In John's Gospel, Jesus' teaching often comes in measured, beautifully constructed speeches. They start with images that are warm and intriguing in which Jesus describes himself. It's easy to pick out occasions when Jesus is about to reveal something important about himself because his statements begin grandly: 'I am.' The original readers would have sensed something Godlike in that. For instance, Jesus compares himself to a vine and his followers to its branches. (It's a long section that begins at John 15.1.) The way they would find their strength would be by staying closely attached to him, and they would need that godly strength in order to be people of love when life got difficult.

In Matthew's Gospel, much of Jesus' teaching is edited together into a long sermon. Known as the Sermon on the Mount, it covers prayer, revenge, worry, divorce, oaths, fasting, hatred, poverty and how to distinguish truth from lies. Surely that can't have been delivered in one bombardment! It feels more like memorable highlights from three years' worth of sermons brought together for dramatic impact. Fantastic stuff, which you can find in Matthew 5—7.

In Luke's Gospel, Jesus loves to tell a story. The same is true of Matthew and Mark, but Luke has some corkers. The proper name for these stories that make a point is *parables*. In one of them Jesus delivers a full-on attack on greed. (You can find it in Luke 12.16–21.) In the story a rich farmer has a spectacularly good harvest. Overjoyed at his good luck, he rips down his old barns and builds enormous new ones in which to store the grain mountain. With the project complete, he sits down and realizes that he will never have to work again. All he needs to do is enjoy himself for ever, but that night he has a stroke, dies, and that's that. Jesus' zaps the audience with the punchline: 'This is how it will be with those who store up things for themselves but are not rich towards God.'

Jesus hardly ever explained the meaning of his parables. His punchlines, which were challenging, unexpected or beautiful, hung in the air for his listeners to make of them what they chose. The result is that they are still hanging there unexplained in the Gospels as we read them 20 centuries later. So in this parable Jesus might have had a particular individual in mind, or an empire, or an entire economic system. Uncomfortably, he might have been thinking about someone like you. Or you might read it and decide that Jesus must have meant something altogether different. That is the option he left us with.

And Mark's Gospel – what kind of narrator was he? Well, 2,000 years before media-savvy politicians found themselves in front of microphones, Mark loved a soundbite. In fact, at the very beginning of his Gospel, he summarized the whole of Jesus' teaching in three punchy sentences: 'The time has come. The kingdom of God is near. Repent and believe the good news!' Absolutely everything that Jesus taught comes under one of those headlines. (You can find them in Mark 1.15.) Jesus could have put the whole thing in a tweet, and still have had room for an emoji. But 2,000 years have gone by and today's readers need a bit more explanation of what Jesus was driving at. So that's what this chapter is about.

Jesus was Jewish, and in many ways he taught like a typical Jewish leader of the first century. Everything he said was saturated with ideas from the Jewish Scriptures (or as Christians know it, the Old Testament) with its prophecies and regulations. His genius, though, was to scour away the grunge that had accumulated over the years. He gave old ideas new teeth. He revealed the love and justice of God that were still glittering underneath. And he was vicious about the way religious conventions that were originally intended to lead people into godliness had rusted up.

So when Jesus announced, 'The time has come!' he wanted people to know that the coming of the Messiah, the great leader for whom the Jews had longed for centuries, was imminent. The day the Scriptures had anticipated, when God would intervene decisively in human history, was very close. There were several ways that the Old Testament described the Messiah – a shepherd, a servant, a conqueror. Jesus refused to be drawn on whether he claimed to be the Messiah. He told his followers to look at what was happening and make up their own mind, but he made a point of distancing himself from those who wanted him to be a military hero who would overthrow the Roman army. Instead he saw himself in the role of a servant to vulnerable people. Everything he said was geared towards making life better for the poor.

The concept of 'the kingdom of God' was also familiar to those who first listened to Jesus' teaching, but he made it absolutely central to his message. It wasn't a physical place and it wasn't a particular group of people. Jesus used it as a way of describing what the world is like when God is accepted as king and obeyed.

He was too charismatic to bore people with a list of rules that need to be obeyed in God's kingdom. Instead Jesus used parables and invited people to work it out.

When you are in the kingdom it feels like a woman who has been abused and hasn't got a hope, but keeps on and on at a powerful judge until unexpectedly she gets justice. So that's a reason to keep praying.

When you are in the kingdom it feels like you've found a pearl for sale in the market so dazzling that it's worth selling your home and every single possession to buy it. Even if you're left only with the clothes you stand up in, you'll have the pearl and that will be the best decision you ever made. That's how much God matters.

When you're in the Kingdom it feels like you're at the most awesome party. The A-listers turned down the invitation, so the poor, the suffering and the refugees are living it up instead. Society's usual priorities are completely overturned.

All this was deeply controversial to the Pharisees, the group of strict Jews who were mentioned in the last chapter. There is no denying that they were good people. They believed that the calamity that the Jews were experiencing, oppressed by the Roman Empire, had come about because they had disobeyed God's laws in the Old Testament. But because several centuries had passed since the rules were written down and new developments had introduced new ways of doing wrong, the Pharisees were intent on filling in the gaps. They were trying to devise a religious code that covered every circumstance a Jew could possibly find himself or herself in. They cracked down hard on anyone who didn't fulfil their duties.

Jesus loathed them. There's no polite way of putting that, really. The names he called the Pharisees were highly offensive, but he seems to have got away with it because they were funny too. Snake-infested orifices! Luxury coffins! It was their hypocrisy he couldn't stand, especially when they used some detail of the law as an excuse not to inconvenience themselves by being generous or compassionate.

Jesus taught that what God longs for is not a change of behaviour but a change of heart. In the kingdom people would do good not because it was their duty but because they loved other people so much that doing good was a natural response. One of the ways he antagonized the Pharisees was by doing things on the Sabbath that evidently improved the lives of people who were suffering but were strictly speaking contrary to the rules. Which was more important, compassion or legalism?

> 'A new command I give you: Love one another. As I have loved you, so you must love one another. By this everyone will know that you are my disciples, if you love one another.'

And even more aggravating for patriotic Jewish leaders was Jesus' insistence that you could not be regarded as a loving person if you only loved your fellow Jews. God's love extended to the whole of humankind. And his followers needed to do the same. This was one of his most extreme statements, which is startling when you remember that his audience was routinely abused by an army that had overrun their land:

> 'I tell you who hear me: Love your enemies, do good to those who hate you, bless those who curse you, pray for those who ill-treat you. If someone strikes you on one cheek, turn the other also.'

You can find those quotations from Jesus in John 13.34–35 and Luke 6.27–29.

Jesus isn't recorded as saying much about sex, and nothing about homosexuality. (It's not wise, though, to assume that because he was silent on a particular issue Jesus must have shared your own opinion.) When he did talk about sex, it was to make a passionate plea against the misery brought about by adultery. Against the culture of the time, it was the pain caused to women by men sleeping around on which he focused. He had a very poor opinion of men lusting over women, so if you want to make a guess about what he would have thought of internet porn, have a look at Matthew 5.27–30 and remember what the second chapter of this book suggested about exegesis (thinking about the original context) and hermeneutics (translating the values from that original context to today's circumstances).

An issue that featured greatly in Jesus' teaching and hasn't gone away is money. The reason money is dangerous is that it creates the illusion that it's the most important thing in a person's life. There's only room for one king in the kingdom (Luke 16.13): 'You cannot be a slave to both God and Money.' Jesus said that the thing that would most improve a rich person's life was to give away everything he or she had to the poor, and follow his way instead.

It was poor people who really knew what it meant to be blessed, because God knew what they needed and it would be provided. With God given absolute priority in their lives, they would be the first and foremost in the kingdom. It was natural for people to worry about having a roof over their head or clothes to wear, but if they trusted God he would not let them down or leave them to starve.

How did the poor respond to this? They absolutely lapped it up! But the Gospel of John tells us that they were less likely to hang around when the teaching got really complicated and the food ran out.

However, the biggest challenge was the third soundbite: 'Repent and believe the good news.' The kingdom about which Jesus taught would only come about if people took action. 'Repent' means turn around. Jesus asked for a complete change of direction from his followers. Like him, they were to see themselves as God's children.

Their lives must carry the DNA of Jesus, the one who called God 'Father'. They must seek justice wherever it is denied. They must bring about peace. They must be generous, and love people unconditionally. They must have a selfless lifestyle, so much so that commitment to Jesus' mission should be even more important than their family ties.

Jesus used two phrases to describe how his followers were going to be so distinctive that they made improvements to their culture. One was 'the salt of the earth'. Salt was a preservative and the point of his followers' lives was now to preserve society from becoming corrupt. The other was 'the light of the world'. A race that was in moral darkness needed them to illuminate a new path.

Jesus was frank about the fact that those who held power would find this threatening. His friends would be persecuted because of it. They might even die. So why on earth would they follow Jesus? Because, he claimed, he was a different kind of leader from anyone who had gone before. He would be utterly committed to their well-being and he would love them with a passion greater than anything they had previously experienced. Every other leader was in it for what he could get out of it, but Jesus' followers would experience an unprecedented adventure (John 10.10): 'I have come that they may have life, and have it to the full.'

What's more, being in this new community which had turned its back on possessions and embraced love instead was not just going to improve their time on earth. The ultimate reason for following Jesus was that the exhilarating life he offered them would endure for ever. The new relationship they had with God would never end. After death, their lives with Jesus would continue in the presence of God throughout all eternity.

The way of servanthood and sacrifice to which Jesus called people was as challenging a life as it was possible to imagine. But there was a twist.

Eternal life was not something they had to strain with every fibre to earn by doing good. It was God's gift. There was no standard of behaviour they had to exceed. It was free. God's love for humankind was so great that he would give this eternal life to anyone who wanted it. (Elsewhere in the Bible this extraordinary love of God is called 'grace'.)

In fact, an arduous effort to keep every tiny detail of the rules might become an obstacle, as it had for the Pharisees. God himself would do everything that was required to ensure that the human beings for whom he cared so much would receive ever-lasting life.

The best way to come to God was not by producing evidence of the good you had done, but by humbly admitting that you needed his mercy because of all you had failed to do. In fact, the best way to think about relating to God was to come like a tiny child. When you admitted you were helpless and utterly dependent, that was the moment when you were most useful to God. That was when God the Father could create something new and good and never-ending.

Receive God's love which expects nothing in return, Jesus taught. Surrender yourself totally to be cared for like a baby in the very first moments of his or her life. It's like being born again.

BARE NECESSITIES!

This story told by Jesus is greatly loved by Christians. It is often called the parable of the prodigal son ('prodigal' meaning, in this case, a wastrel). It comes from Luke 15.11–24:

> 'There was a man who had two sons. The younger one said to his father, "Father, give me my share of the estate." So he divided his property between them.
>
> 'Not long after that, the younger son got together all he had, set off for a distant country and there squandered his wealth in wild living. After he had spent everything, there was a severe famine in that whole country, and he began to be in need. So he went and hired himself out to a citizen of that country, who sent him to his fields to feed pigs. He longed to fill his stomach with the pods that the pigs were eating, but no one gave him anything.

'When he came to his senses, he said, "How many of my father's hired servants have food to spare, and here I am starving to death! I will set out and go back to my father and say to him: Father, I have sinned against heaven and against you. I am no longer worthy to be called your son; make me like one of your hired servants." So he got up and went to his father.

'But while he was still a long way off, his father saw him and was filled with compassion for him; he ran to his son, threw his arms around him and kissed him.

'The son said to him, "Father, I have sinned against heaven and against you. I am no longer worthy to be called your son."

'But the father said to his servants, "Quick! Bring the best robe and put it on him. Put a ring on his finger and sandals on his feet. Bring the fattened calf and kill it. Let's have a feast and celebrate. For this son of mine was dead and is alive again; he was lost and is found." So they began to celebrate.'

The Gospels almost never record Jesus explaining his parables. Instead, he tells the tale and leaves those who hear it to work out what they make of it. In that spirit, assuming that the father represents God, what do you make of this story?

BARELY MORE!

A varied selection from Jesus' teaching can be found in Luke 13.18—15.32. There are some very short parables that invite people to imagine the impact of the kingdom of God. Jesus gives daunting challenges to those who think being one of his followers is an easy option. There are examples of what humility looks like in practice. And there are three tender stories that affirm God's love for those who, in the world's eyes, are 'lost'. This section finishes with an unexpected sequel to the parable of the prodigal son in which his older brother complains that being debauched and then turning back to God seems to be a better deal than living a moral life all along.

It's the twenty-first century. This teaching of Jesus does not seem to have lost any of its clout. Being a follower of Jesus was originally costly. Then for a long period during which respectable people went to church it turned into something cosy. In recent years it has reverted to being costly again.

What do you think is going on?

UNCOVERED!

Keep reading to the end of Luke's Gospel. Extracts from Jesus' teaching continue until the end of chapter 21. The last of those chapters includes statements he made in Jerusalem during the final week of his life, and it is clear why he became an increasingly controversial figure. Then comes the emotional account of Jesus' death and resurrection.

5 Letters to churches and Christians

You know how frustrating it is when someone on a train is speaking to someone on the phone and it's evident that the person on the other end is having an affair but you can't hear the details of that half of the conversation? That's how I feel about the 21 letters in the New Testament.

They were all written in response to something really important that was going on in someone's life or a predicament in a church 20 years or so after Jesus. We have the response, but we don't know what it was that prompted the letters to be written. We need to work it out from the part of the conversation that we've got.

About half of those letters (or epistles, to give their old-fashioned name) are signed by a man called Paul. He was one of the most significant Christian leaders in the second half of the first century. It's not certain that he actually wrote all the letters that are ascribed to him. He was such a towering figure that theologians think a couple of them may have been written in the style of Paul, and his name got added so that when they were copied and circulated they would have authority.

So what was it about this man that was so imposing that the people who compiled the New Testament tried to include every scrap of his writing they could find? His story is told in a book called the Acts of the Apostles (or just Acts). It's by the same author as the Gospel of Luke, and it's a sequel to the tumultuous events of Jesus' life.

Jesus' last instructions to his followers were that they should wait in Jerusalem and expect something that would make them immensely powerful. They did, meeting together regularly to pray. Of the 12 close followers that Jesus chose, 11 were still alive (these were the Apostles of the book's title). A few dozen others, including many women, were part of that group as well.

Jerusalem was packed because the Jewish harvest festival, Pentecost, was taking place, but something unprecedented happened to the followers of Jesus. Their prayer meeting turned passionately ecstatic. It attracted a crowd and Jesus' friend Peter made a speech. He announced that this was the moment of power they had been waiting for. The Spirit of God had been given to them in an overwhelming way.

The Jews were familiar with the idea of God being present in the world through his Holy Spirit, but this was way beyond anything that had happened before. Peter declared that it was proof that Jesus was the Messiah they had been waiting for. His death has been a terrible thing, but he had been raised again to life. This Holy Spirit was the way Jesus would be recognized in the world from now on. Peter urged the crowd to seek forgiveness for their part in Jesus' death, and to believe in him as the Messiah – different from and greater than anything they had anticipated.

Three thousand or so people believed it and joined the followers of Jesus. Suddenly it was a huge, confident group. They lived as Jesus had taught them. They shared their resources, worked for the good of those who were ill or poor, met together joyfully, and worshipped him as God. It was idyllic. And as the visiting Jews returned from Jerusalem to their home countries, they took the story and the teaching of Jesus with them.

The Jewish leaders had assumed that this Jesus-obsessed sect would die along with him. So when they saw it growing, they took action to end it. There were threats, imprisonments and murders. Those who could do so escaped to safe towns, but it didn't stop them believing that Jesus was the Messiah, with the result that little groups of believers were worshipping him in towns all round the Mediterranean.

This is where Paul came in. He was known as Saul in those days and was one of the Jews' finest intellectuals. They employed him to travel widely, imprison the people who were calling themselves the Followers of the Way, and stamp out the Jesus sect. Big mistake!

Paul's vendetta took him on a journey north from Jerusalem. He was carrying arrest warrants for Jesus' followers, but he had a sudden and terrifying vision, which flung him to the ground and temporarily blinded him. He was convinced he had come face to face with the living Jesus. He was helped to Damascus, where he announced to the astonished worshippers of Jesus that he was now a believer. His sight returned and, for his own protection, he was spirited away to his home town of Tarsus (in modern-day Turkey).

He set about rigorously studying the Jewish Scriptures (the Old Testament). He became certain that Jesus was the Messiah and that his coming had been foreseen centuries before. He was to become the most significant theologian of his era. He also became the most widely travelled missionary of his day, because he was determined that all the major towns around the north coast of the Mediterranean Sea should have an opportunity to hear the story of Jesus. His greatest ambition was to be able to stand in Rome, the heart of the known world, and preach that God had touched the world in the person of Jesus.

He succeeded, and the impact was world-changing. With their chief persecutor now worshipping with them, the Christians (as they were now calling themselves) had a period of peace. Small churches established themselves over a wide area. Many of them were founded by Paul and his companions. A typical pattern was that he would stay in a town until he was confident that there were leaders in place who could sustain the group's life of worship and service, and then move on to start the process somewhere else. He kept in touch with the churches he had founded by letters, delivered by hand by his companions. That is what we now have as epistles to the churches in Galatia (Galatians), Corinth (1 Corinthians and, a couple of years later, 2 Corinthians), and so on.

The point of the letters was to unpack the significance of the fact that, in the person of Jesus, God had walked and talked on the planet. As a result, God and humankind could be reconciled in a completely unprecedented way. The fact was so mind-blowing (and still is) that it needed detailed and complex explanation.

During this time a completely unexpected development took place. Gentiles (people who were not Jewish) were also becoming convinced that Jesus had risen from the dead and was God. Paul was the ideal person to manage the immense transformation that would be involved in incorporating these new believers. Much of the content of the letters is therefore about who Jesus actually was. He was far more than the politically astute, miracle-working teacher who first inspired a group of Jewish fishermen. His life, death and resurrection had brought about the salvation of the entire world. All that was needed was faith that this was so.

You can imagine the people to whom the letters were addressed sitting in a room or courtyard of a first-century house listening to it being read. They can't have been a huge crowd because they were constrained by the size of the space. They would have dwelt on every word, because they were hearing for the first time concepts that Christians have now had 20 centuries to reflect on. Undoubtedly they took delight in references to individuals, because there were many personal greetings. They would surely have needed the words read more than once, because the ideas are so complicated. And it's highly likely that one of the more educated ones would have made a copy so that the letter could be circulated to other towns.

Other letters in the New Testament were not written to specific people, but to Christians scattered through what would now be known as the Middle East. They have names like the Letter to the Hebrews, or the Letter of James. These were written a couple of decades later. One of the themes that's repeated is the need for trust in Jesus as the persecution of Christians became more common. They show God reaching out to a needy world with immeasurable love. They put right misunderstandings about the nature of Jesus and have practical advice on how to live as his followers.

One aspect of the New Testament that will always be frus-trating is that neither Paul nor any of the other authors definitively wrote, 'This is what the Christian faith is.' All the letters give vital fragments of it, responding to what people in different places needed to know at that moment. The business of making it coherent has fallen to preachers over the last 2,000 years. Different church leaders have emphasized different elements. The glorious pieces of the mosaic have been arranged in various ways. This is one of the reasons the world's 2 billion Christians are gathered into various groups (called denominations) who share one New Testament but have come to slightly different conclusions about the implications of what they read there.

To work out without help what was going on in each location is a struggle. Alongside each letter, you need a book to read that explains why Paul and the others chose to write about particular subjects. Such books do exist: they are called commentaries. However, even commentaries are forced to admit that there are some references that are so obscure that theologians just make a guess about what they mean.

There are a number of issues that were obviously very significant in the first century, but have ceased to be an issue in the twenty-first century. There are other issues that are timeless and vital to shaping the world that God longs for today, but it's difficult to be sure which is which. For instance, Paul poses this question: 'Does not the very nature of things teach you that if a man has long hair, it is a disgrace to him, but that if a woman has long hair, it is her glory?'

Well Paul, no! Frankly, it doesn't. It clearly did in your generation, and we utterly respect that, but the nature of things has changed since you posed your question in 1 Corinthians 11.14–15. Our generation is gelled, highlighted, plaited, dreadlocked, cropped, dyed and quiffed because our culture has a different set of expectations. Out of respect for what you have written, we will try to work out what concern the people of Corinth had. What did they say to you in the silent half of the conversation to which your letter was a reply? (That's exegesis.)

I reckon the issue that was unsettling them is that when Christians meet together to worship, no fashion trend should be such a big deal that it becomes more important than praising God. That would make sense of your words. It's also an enduring principle. We too need to work out how we are going to do that in a way that makes sense for our generation. (That's hermeneutics.)

In other places Paul gives instructions that appear to apply only to the first century but have unchanging implications. For instance, while Paul was writing to those hairy Christians in Corinth, a famine had plunged Jerusalem into distress. Christians had to consider something that had never occurred to them before. As followers of Jesus, were they responsible for needy people if they didn't know them and they lived in places they would never visit?

Paul's answer was yes. He established a fundraising system in which money was regularly and generously set aside by those who had plenty. It was then transported safely and with precautions against fraud to those who were suffering. His letter had in mind a unique situation. So should Christians of the twenty-first century still be using those principles in a world that is bigger and more unequal than Paul could ever have conceived? Hell, yeah!

I can't pretend that navigating these letters is going to be easy. You really do need to bear in mind that there was a specific context for which they were written, and it is different from today's. From our perspective it's now difficult to understand why the letter writers were so agitated about obscure philosophies that were leading people away from faith in Jesus.

It's worth persisting, however, because of the times when, with great beauty and simplicity, the glory of what God did for humankind in the life, death and resurrection of Jesus was explained for the very first time. This is Romans 8.37–39:

> We are more than conquerors through him who loved us. For I am convinced that neither death nor life, neither angels nor demons, neither the present nor the future, nor any powers, neither height nor depth, nor anything else in all creation, will be able to separate us from the love of God that is in Christ Jesus our Lord.

BARE NECESSITIES!

This is also from Paul's letter to the church in Rome, written in about 56. It's an extract that begins with what seems to be a quote from a popular hymn. Singing in praise of God featured in the worship of Christians from the very start – just as it had in the worship of Jews before them. Then Paul goes on to write, 'If that's true, so what?' First of all he describes how Christians should behave when they are together in a church service. Then he goes on to explain how the followers of Jesus should live distinctive lifestyles from Monday to Saturday. He blows apart any suggestion that, for a Christian, religion should be a private thing. It's a call to have values that are noticeably different from society's norms. It comes from Romans 11.33—12.18:

> Oh, the depth of the riches of the wisdom and knowledge
>   of God!
> How unsearchable his judgments,
> and his paths beyond tracing out!

'Who has known the mind of the Lord?
Or who has been his counsellor?'
'Who has ever given to God,
that God should repay the gift?'
For from him and through him and to him are all things.
To him be the glory for ever! Amen.

Therefore, I urge you, brothers and sisters, in view of God's mercy, to offer your bodies as living sacrifices, holy and pleasing to God – this is your spiritual act of worship. Do not conform to the pattern of this world, but be transformed by the renewing of your mind. Then you will be able to test and approve what God's will is – his good, pleasing and perfect will.

For by the grace given me I say to every one of you: Do not think of yourself more highly than you ought, but rather think of yourself with sober judgment, in accordance with the measure of faith God has given you. Just as each of us has one body with many members, and these members do not all have the same function, so in Christ we who are many form one body, and each member belongs to all the others. We have different gifts, according to the grace given us. If your gift is prophesying, then use it in proportion to your faith. If it is serving, then serve; if it is teaching, then teach; if it is encouraging, then encourage; if it is contributing to the needs of others, then give generously; if it is leadership, then govern diligently; if it is showing mercy, then do it cheerfully.

Love must be sincere. Hate what is evil; cling to what is good. Be devoted to one another with mutual affection. Honour one another above yourselves. Never be lacking in zeal, but keep your spiritual fervour, serving the Lord.

Be joyful in hope, patient in affliction, faithful in prayer. Share with God's people who are in need. Practise hospitality.

Bless those who persecute you; bless and do not curse. Rejoice with those who rejoice; mourn with those who mourn. Live in harmony with one another. Do not be proud, but be willing to associate with people of low position. Do not be conceited.

Do not repay anyone evil for evil. Be careful to do what is right in the eyes of everybody. If it is possible, as far as it depends on you, live at peace with everyone.

I guess Paul's list of the different gifts that people have could have gone on for ever. He never mentioned being good at medicine, let alone IT.

So, in that spirit, what are you good at? What are you doing with it to benefit others?

BARELY MORE!

Read Paul's letter to the church at Philippi (it's just called Philippians in most Bibles). It will take less time than changing a bed and you'll love it.

Paul and his young assistant Timothy visited Philippi, which is in Greece, in about 50. Paul got himself into a load of trouble and found himself in jail. He astonished the authorities by not escaping when he had an easy opportunity, preferring to stay and talk to people about Jesus. Several families converted to Christianity before he travelled on. Twelve years later Paul found himself in prison again somewhere else (this wasn't unusual for him). He wrote this very personal letter to the families who now made up the small church he had founded.

I chose it because it's typical of letters that Paul wrote, but you don't need a lot of cultural background explained. They all have a similar structure: a greeting and some personal information, teaching about the history and nature of Jesus, practical instructions about how Christians should live as followers of Jesus, and a tender goodbye.

The one thing it will help you to know is that when Paul rails against circumcision, he's not angry about either female genital mutilation or male surgical procedures. The thing that infuriated him was a group of people who wrongly insisted that if you were a Gentile who wanted to become a Christian you had to become Jewish as well, with all the rituals that involved.

You will come away knowing that Paul adored Jesus, loved the Christians he was writing to, and wanted Jesus' followers to take joy in making the world a better place. You can entertain yourself by guessing which filthy Greek word is translated as 'rubbish' in English Bibles. Naughty step, Paul!

Pick out one phrase about the character of Jesus that you warm to, and one phrase about how Christians should live distinctive lives. Turn them round in your mind for a while, thinking about the implications.

UNCOVERED!

More than any other kind of literature in the Bible, it's difficult to recommend a letter to read. There are obscure ideas that only made sense centuries ago, and you really need to read the letters alongside a commentary that explains them.

However, I think you might get on well with 1 John. (There are three letters quite close to the end of the Bible that are associated with John − 1 John is the first of the three.) It's different from Paul's letters, which were written to a particular group of people. There is no indication to whom 1 John is addressed or by whom it's written. Instead it has a timeless feel, as if it was meant for all Christians in all times and places.

If you come across a phrase that begins with a capital (such as Word of Life or Righteous One), just assume it's about Jesus. It does get a bit complicated, because the author was trying to explain why some ideas about Jesus that were floating round were missing the point. When it gets to the climax, about how there is no fear in love and God's absolute love will drive your fear away, you'll find it inspirational.

6 Timeless stories

Take your imagination way back into history. Maybe 600 years before Jesus; maybe even before. Sit yourself among the members of a large extended family around a fire.

It is the time of evening when the day's work is done, a meal has been eaten and stories are told. Tonight it's the turn of everyone's favourite storyteller. The story he tells has been told many times before. It is a story of God and humans. It is a warning tale about how it's possible to be so overcome with your own ambition that you think you are God's equal.

The tale begins: 'Long ago all the people of earth lived together in one place. Their great longing was to do something that would never, ever be forgotten. So they decided to build a tower that would rise so high into the sky that they could reach out and touch God. They baked bricks and began to build.

'However, God knew that such a thing would bring no good. If we are to thrive he must not be our equal, but our Lord. So to stop them completing the tower, God plunged the people into confusion. Every tribe among them started to speak in a different way. They couldn't understand each other. They couldn't even trust each other, let alone build a tower together. So the people scattered all over the earth, and from that time onwards every tribe speaks its own language.'

The children around the fire shiver because they have seen a tower such as that – a ziggurat all in ruins. 'Is it true?' they ask.

The storyteller doesn't really answer the question. Perhaps it's such an old story that he doesn't know. He does know, though, that the story is full of truths about God. He smiles because tonight he has a new twist to add to the story. He has invented a name for the tower. It's a name that sounds a bit like the confused babble of different languages, but it also sounds a bit like the family's deadly enemy – the nation of Babylon.

He takes a deep breath and concludes: 'And the name of that terrible tower is Babel.'

The first chapters of the Bible contain timeless stories such as these. They are stories saturated with truth, but the truths they uncover about God are so profound and meaningful that mere factual writing could not convey their seriousness. So the writing is designed to work luxuriantly on our imaginations. The technical term for these stories is 'myth'. A myth is so steeped in meaning that a scientific or historical account could never tell us so much truth.

The first book of the Bible is called Genesis. It starts with a jaw-dropping acclamation of the creativity of God. Everything that exists, from dust to DNA, is there because of God's good plan. Then there is a story of a man and a woman, which helps us reflect on how this world of breathtaking beauty became a place in which humans suffer at each other's hands. After the myth of Adam and Eve and their children comes the saga of Noah and the vessel in which God saved him from a devastating flood.

The resolute truth of this story is that evil will not have the last word, because those who trust in God have an eternal destiny that is unshakeable. The story of the tower called Babel comes in Genesis 11.1–9.

After Genesis 12, some readers identify a change of tone. It's the beginning of the story of Abraham (or Abram), to whom the Jews (or, as they were more accurately called at the time, the Hebrews) looked as their ancestor. The language increasingly makes us feel that we are in the hands of a historian as much as the hands of a storyteller. The rip-roaring stories of the generations that followed (Abraham's son Isaac, and his grandsons Jacob and Esau) seem to have some of the qualities of a myth and some of a researched narrative. There are stories of love, rivalry, tragedy and reconciliation. They seem to be teaching us something timeless about our lives, but also leading us into something recognizable as a history of God's people.

Other stories in the Old Testament have a mythological feel similar to its opening chapters. For instance, a long poem, howling with pain about why terrible things can happen to good people, is topped and tailed with the story of Job. It tells how Satan taunts God with the accusation that as soon as people experience tragedy they stop worshipping him. God allows Satan to bring calamity on Job but, despite suffering and doubt, Job's trust that there is a God of love remains.

The majority of Christians read these timeless stories in the spirit in which they were first told and retold. However, it must be added that some Christians feel strongly that the first chapters of the Bible should be accepted as revealing a more 'literal' truth about the origins of the cosmos. From those narratives they build an alternative to mainstream science in which the universe is younger and smaller than is generally accepted. In Europe this group is tiny, but vocal. In the developing world it is larger. And there are some schools and museums (notably in the USA) in which 'creation science' is presented as factual.

Traditionally, Jews and Christians named Moses as the author of the ancient stories of Genesis, and the books of Exodus, Leviticus, Numbers and Deuteronomy which follow. Together the first five books of the Bible are called the Pentateuch (it means 'five scrolls') and they form the heart of what Jews call the Torah.

For the past hundred years, however, most people have assumed that the names of the people who told and wrote down these wonderful stories are lost in history. It is usually reckoned that the version we read today was edited together from several different sources in the sixth century BC.

Theologians try to unpick the strands of the edited version. They suggest that there are four authors (or more probably four schools of thought) whose writings have been edited together. They are known as the Elohist, the Yahwist, the Priest and the Deuteronomist. They can be identified by the different names and characteristics they give to God. Each of them had a different purpose in writing. The fact that there are different authors explains why there are repetitions and changes of tone.

The place where this is first obvious is Genesis 2.4, where the Bible seems to begin all over again. The Priestly writer, whose presentation of God is awesome and barely describable, was responsible for the first chapter. The Yahwist, whose presentation of God is almost human, with legs and breath and emotions, wrote chapter 2. Much later, they were put side by side.

People who study for a theology degree at university sometimes spend their first term working out which writer was responsible for each chapter of the Old Testament, but side by side, these accounts have been part of Jewish and then Christian Scripture for 26 centuries. Scholarship keeps revealing new possibilities, and during the last 30 years academics have tended to stress the similarities between the strands rather than the differences.

BARE NECESSITIES!

Now that you can put it in context, read the opening words of the Bible. They come from Genesis 1.1—2.3. What do they help believers understand about the 4.5 billion years during which our wonderful blue-green blob has been orbiting the sun?

In the beginning God created the heavens and the earth. Now the earth was formless and empty, darkness was over the surface of the deep, and the Spirit of God was hovering over the waters.

And God said, 'Let there be light,' and there was light. God saw that the light was good, and he separated the light from the darkness. God called the light 'day', and the darkness he called 'night'. And there was evening, and there was morning – the first day.

And God said, 'Let there be an expanse between the waters to separate water from water.' So God made the expanse and separated the water under the expanse from the water above it. And it was so. God called the expanse 'sky'. And there was evening, and there was morning – the second day.

And God said, 'Let the water under the sky be gathered to one place, and let dry ground appear.' And it was so. God called the dry ground 'land', and the gathered waters he called 'seas'. And God saw that it was good.

Then God said, 'Let the land produce vegetation: seed-bearing plants and trees on the land that bear fruit with seed in it, according to their various kinds.' And it was so. The land produced vegetation: plants bearing seed according to their kinds and trees bearing fruit with seed in it according to their kinds. And God saw that it was good. And there was evening, and there was morning – the third day.

And God said, 'Let there be lights in the expanse of the sky to separate the day from the night, and let them serve as signs to mark sacred times, and days and years, and let them be lights in the expanse of the sky to give light on the earth.' And it was so. God made two great lights – the greater light to govern the day and the lesser light to govern the night. He also made the stars. God set them in the expanse of the sky to give light on the earth, to govern the day and the night, and to separate light from darkness. And God saw that it was good. And there was evening, and there was morning – the fourth day.

And God said, 'Let the water teem with living creatures, and let birds fly above the earth across the expanse of the sky.' So God created the great creatures of the sea and every living thing with which the water teems and that moves about in it, according to their kinds, and every winged bird according to its kind. And God saw that it was good. God blessed them and said, 'Be fruitful and increase in number and fill the water in the seas, and let the birds increase on the earth.' And there was evening, and there was morning – the fifth day.

And God said, 'Let the land produce living creatures according to their kinds: the livestock, the creatures that move along the ground, and the wild animals, each according to its kind.' And it was so. God made the wild animals according to their kinds, the livestock according to their kinds, and all the creatures that move along the ground according to their kinds. And God saw that it was good.

Then God said, 'Let us make human beings in our image, in our likeness, so that they may rule over the fish in the sea and the birds in the sky, over the livestock and all the wild animals, and over all the creatures that move along the ground.'

So God created human beings
in his own image,
in the image of God
he created them;
male and female
he created them.

God blessed them and said to them, 'Be fruitful and increase in number; fill the earth and subdue it. Rule over the fish in the sea and the birds in the sky and over every living creature that moves on the ground.'

Then God said, 'I give you every seed-bearing plant on the face of the whole earth and every tree that has fruit with seed in it. They will be yours for food. And to all the beasts of the earth and all the birds in the sky and all the creatures that move along the ground – everything that has the breath of life in it – I give every green plant for food.' And it was so.

God saw all that he had made, and it was very good. And there was evening, and there was morning – the sixth day. Thus the heavens and the earth were completed in all their vast array.

By the seventh day God had finished the work he had been doing; so on the seventh day he rested from all his work. Then God blessed the seventh day and made it holy, because on it he rested from all the work of creating that he had done.

If we set on one aside the possibility that this timeless story might be trying to teach us science, here is a different list of things it wants to teach us.

- There is a clear pattern to this account. Everything is in equilibrium. On day one there is light, and then on day four there are suns and stars. On day two there is air and water, and on day five they are full of birds and fish. Then on day three there is land and greenery, while on day six it is inhabited by animals and humans. This interdependence of animals, plants and minerals in a delicate balance is what might nowadays be termed ecology.
- The world is not in the hands of impersonal forces controlling humankind. (Bad news for horoscope fans!) It is in the hands of a God whose intentions are described as good, good, good, good, good and very good.
- There aren't a thousand little gods bickering over how our world should be, but one. In some ways that is the most significant message of the Old Testament. The Hebrew people doubted it again and again.
- The material world around us is not an evil thing, above which we need to rise. The reason we seek God is not to escape the world with its delicious tastes, glorious sights and sexy joys. These things are good (times six).
- There is, and always has been, a plan.

BARELY MORE!

Read the story of Noah's ark, beloved of children's story books and toy shops. It is told in Genesis 6.5—9.17. Two things will quickly become obvious – the animals have a peripheral role, and the original story is entirely unsuitable for children.

A tale similar to this appears in other ancient religious texts as well. For instance, in the Hindu chronicle *Matsya Purana* the god Vishnu arranges for virtuous Manu to escape a deluge in a huge boat. And the *Epic of Gilgamesh* from Mesopotamia has a version so similar to the one you are reading that many people think the Bible account, many centuries later, must have been based on it.

The idea that unwavering trust in God will save those who are dismayed by the wickedness of the world around them appears ingrained in a religious view of the world. Writers of the New Testament saw the ark as a symbol of the Christian Church, in which the followers of Jesus travel together towards resurrection.

It is necessary to acknowledge, though, that some Christians have a sincere belief in Noah as an historical character and the global flood as a verifiable event. During the twentieth century this prompted archaeological expeditions seeking the location. They proved disappointing.

Below are some thoughts that you might carry with you as you read about Noah.

The thrust of the narrative is that human beings are capable of behaving in appalling ways, but evil will not have the final word. Those who trust in God have a destiny that is secure and eternal. Who might find this a story of hope, and for whom is it a story of condemnation?

What was it about Noah that would have made the original hearers think, 'I need to be like him?'

UNCOVERED!

Read the whole of Genesis 1.1—12.8 to sweep through some irresistible stories that share a 'mythological' quality. Some of the timeless questions on which these stories shine a light are these (although they never fully answer them).

- Why does life exist?
- Why do human beings come in two equally wonderful shapes?
- Why is life so darned hard?
- Why do we do terrible things to each other?
- Can faith in God rescue us, and if so from what?

Skip the list of names and ages, but in chapter 12 the story of Abraham will just get going (Abram was his original name). In his home town of Ur he must have bewildered his neighbours because he had two revelations that made him absolutely unique in that place. There is only one God. And that God is invisible. The ideas are so familiar to us that it's easy to miss their significance, but, ye gods, they changed the world! That's what the next chapter is about.

7 A dramatic history

About a quarter of the Bible is devoted to the history of the Jews, and how they came to be established in the land where Jesus was born. The accounts overlap, they are not in chronological order, there are gaps, and they sometimes give contradictory versions of the same event. Good luck!

On the plus side, these narratives are crammed with unforgettable stories. They have been made into films countless times. They were written to show that the whole history of humankind is riddled through with the presence of God, working out his good (although sometimes perplexing) purposes. The stories are deeply precious to Jewish people worldwide. Christians look at them and sense that for thousands of years, because of or despite the rise and fall of empires, God was preparing the world for Jesus.

Here you will find famous stories like Joseph, who had an amazing technicolour dream coat. He was loathed by his brothers for being his father's favourite and they sold him to slave traders. A series of extraordinary twists involves promotion, seduction, jail, an introduction to the Pharaoh, high office and the rescue of a nation facing famine. His brothers end up in front of him, begging for food and unaware of his identity. In a beautifully written scene, we are tantalized as to whether Joseph will use his power to forgive or destroy them. The story is told in Genesis chapters 37 and 39—50.

You will also find virtually unknown but equally thrilling stories like that of Tamar. Buried in the middle of Joseph's story, you can find this in Genesis 38. Some time after her 'wicked' husband has died and other men have acted dishonourably, Tamar disguises herself as a prostitute and sets out to get justice by exposing the man who slept with her and cheated her. In a nail-biting climax she saves herself from execution because (just like Monica Lewinsky at the end of the twentieth century) she has kept some incriminating evidence hidden. A man who behaved badly is disgraced; a woman displays heroism.

So there is plenty here to enjoy. The history of the Jewish people (or the Hebrews, as they were known until about 900 years before Jesus) begins with Abraham. He lived in the region to which we would now give the name Iraq. Unlike almost everyone else of his generation, Abraham believed that there was only one God and that you couldn't use an idol to make God visible. This is the God who is worshipped today by Christians, Jews and Muslims. His beliefs were a startling contrast to his neighbours who worshipped hundreds of gods whom they believed controlled the weather, the crops and so on.

Abraham and his family left their home, a town called Ur, because they were following a compelling call to do so by the God they worshipped. They travelled hundreds of miles and made a new home in the region where Jesus would be born many centuries later ('the Promised Land'). Under a star-filled sky God made a vow to Abraham that he would be the ancestor of a nation as innumerable as the solar system. The sign of that covenant was to be the circumcision of all males – still joyfully significant in

Judaism. Abraham's wife Sarah gave birth at a very advanced age, and they called their son Isaac.

Muslims also revere Abraham and worship the God he loved. By tradition the founder of Islam, Muhammad, is considered to be a descendant of Abraham. While Jews trace their ancestry through Isaac, Muslims see all Arab people as being descended from a different son, named Ishmael.

Abraham's family swelled to a community and then, following battles with their neighbours, a settled tribe. Many years later there was a famine throughout the region. The Hebrew people migrated to Egypt. (This is where the story of Joseph fits. He was Abraham's great-grandson and used his influential position to allow the Hebrew refugees to settle.)

The Hebrew immigrants were welcomed at first, but they became scapegoats for Egypt's misfortunes and were oppressed. They became slaves in the land in which they had taken refuge. However, under the leadership of a man called Moses they were encouraged to rediscover their true identity. Egypt suffered a series of environmental and health catastrophes which ravaged the economy. Increasingly confident that God's hand was in this, the Hebrews defied their oppressors and escaped into the desert. In a miraculous episode known as the exodus, they crossed the Red Sea into freedom. This episode has been celebrated with worship and thanksgiving every year since then in the meal known as the Passover.

For the Hebrews, liberation was the defining moment in their history. A tiny, vulnerable tribe had become a free nation. Moses taught that it had happened because the God of their ancestor Abraham had willed it. He had chosen them because through them he could demonstrate that all the gods worshipped by the world's great empires were worthless. Weak in themselves, they had achieved great things solely because they had a great God. This God was the creator of all things, and the name they were to know him by was YHWH. This name became so sacred to the Hebrews that they could barely utter it. It is sometimes spelled Yahweh and pronounced like breath itself. It means 'I am who I am' (and it implies 'and I have always been and I will always be').

For 40 years the Hebrews were nomads. It was a time of profound learning for them. Life was harsh in the desert. Their leaders constantly reminded them that with the immense privilege of being God's chosen people came responsibilities. The reason they had been chosen was so that the whole of the world would be blessed through them. During these years the Hebrews organized their community life, and their legal system was established. At its heart were the Ten Commandments, which Christians to this day regard as the framework that underpins their ethical values. Stones on which the commandments were engraved were kept in an ornate wooden chest known as the Ark of the Covenant. It became a revered symbol of the presence of God. (This is the treasure that drives the plot of the 1981 film *Raiders of the Lost Ark*.)

The Hebrews' worship was expressed through the sacrifice of animals. It was a sign of gratitude and trust because they were giving away to God their source of food, and they had faith that he would not forsake them. A huge and richly decorated tent called the Tabernacle was the centre of their worship, but at times of hunger and ill health it was not so obvious to them that they were blessed by God. Despite all the evidence, they began to look back to their former wretched circumstances as the good old days.

Moses chose Joshua to succeed him as leader of the people. Under his leadership the Hebrews grew their military strength.

The objective was to retake the land in which Abraham had settled centuries before, a fertile and beautiful place in which they would thrive. The conquest of Canaan was brutal and bloody, but successful. The people dispersed through the land and settled in communities based on their ancestry – tribes named after Joseph and his 11 brothers. They became a significant force in the region, living among those of other nationalities who continued to occupy Canaan. A series of military and religious leaders called judges, both male and female, gave them a shared identity.

The repeated lament of the Bible's account, however, is that the Hebrews adopted the customs of the people among whom they lived. An ongoing source of anguish was that they married those who worshipped other gods, and in times of need were as likely to pray to idols as they were to worship YHWH. The most dangerous of the enemies were the Philistines, who lived in five cities near the Mediterranean coast and repeatedly fought the Hebrews.

It took a monarch to unite the tribes fully as a nation. The Hebrews' last and most revered judge, Samuel, was persuaded to acknowledge the need for a king who would equip a professional army. He chose a man called Saul. Ill with depression, his initial military success gave way to unpredictable behaviour and unwise strategies. His successor King David, who lived about 1,000 years before Jesus, triumphantly united the 12 tribes and began what the Jews regarded as a golden age. His armies captured Jerusalem and he made that the capital city of the kingdom of Israel.

David was a godly man, wildly popular but flawed. He was an adulterer and had such poor relationships within his family that he had to put down a rebellion led by his own son. However, united under David, this was a time when Israel flourished economically and a series of victories made it militarily secure. He was a fine poet, effectively organized a government, and was so significant in collective Jewish memory that for centuries they longed for a new leader who could worthily occupy David's throne. The people who met Jesus centuries later were giving him the highest accolade when they called him 'son of David'.

David was the father of Solomon, who succeeded him and built the first temple to YHWH on Mount Zion in Jerusalem. The Bible portrays him as wise, but increasingly compromised by greed and an astounding sexual appetite. Solomon's son Reheboam, however, reigned in a way that was progressively tyrannical. A civil war became inevitable. It permanently divided those who lived in the north (called Israel) from those who lived around Jerusalem in the south (called Judah). The ten tribal groups in the north were called Israelites, and the others became known as the Jews. This is why up to this point God's people have been referred to as the Hebrews – strictly speaking, the Jews are those who lived in the southern kingdom.

The history books of the Old Testament then catalogue a series of kings, of whom the lamentable ones considerably outnumber the virtuous ones. Usually if a king is acclaimed as righteous it's because he was determined to make obedience to the ways of YHWH central to the nation's life. The ways of God were made plain in the poetry of men and women called prophets, who delivered messages that were sometimes well received but often not. They repeatedly warned against creating pacts with foreign powers that would require acceptance of their gods as part of the alliance.

Regardless of the warnings, alliances were made and broken, idols were erected and destroyed. The worship of the gods Baal and Asherah may have involved child sacrifice and ritual sex, described by the prophets as utterly detestable to God. Eventually Israel (the northern part of the kingdom) was conquered by Assyria. Those of its inhabitants who were not slaughtered became subsumed in that vast empire and never again had a national identity of their own.

In the south of the kingdom, Judah managed to survive for over a century, enduring sieges and bloodshed. Finally it too was overrun by an empire called Babylon. The destruction of Jerusalem was catastrophic. The Ark of the Covenant, which had travelled with them for so long as a revered symbol of God's presence, was lost. All the Jews who might become economically useful as labourers or prostitutes were taken into exile. They experienced eight brutal decades of captivity. They were utterly demoralized. They believed that they had not only lost their homeland but also, buried in the rubble of the shattered Temple, lost their God.

Unexpectedly, though, they began to realize that it would be possible for them to prosper even though they were in exile in Babylon. Some of them had their talent recognized and were given positions of authority, such as Esther and Daniel, whose stories are told in the books named after them.

They began to grasp that God had not died when his Temple was destroyed. He had come with them to Babylon. In fact, he was everywhere in the world. Worship began again, not centred on the Temple but in local synagogues where Jews gathered weekly. It was at this time that their Scriptures began to be collected. Parts of them had existed for many years, but scholars began to edit them and rewrite them to tell coherently the story of God at work in the world. The writings that emerged had a shape that began to look a little like the books we read in the Old Testament.

About half of it has its origin from this time. Most significantly, during those years the expectation grew that a new leader would emerge. He would bring liberation like the days of the exodus, well-being like the days in the Promised Land, and security as in the days of David. They called that leader the Messiah, or the Christ.

Power changed hands in the region and an emperor named Cyrus took control. He began to repatriate the Jews to their homeland. In waves led by Ezra, Nehemiah and Zerubbabel, people returned to where their grandparents had once lived. The last historical narratives of the Old Testament show them rebuilding Jerusalem and re-establishing the farms that would allow them to thrive. The age-old problems of relationships with other ethnic groups had not gone away, but there is optimism in the way the resettlement is described.

Like any history, these stories are written from a particular viewpoint. As far as the writers were concerned, they are not essentially the stories of Abraham and David. They are not even the stories of Israel and Judah. They are the story of YHWH and his purposes for the world he created. None of the writers ever adds, 'And now I will tell you the meaning of this story.' Occasionally events unfold in a way that points us to something important about God. (For instance, a phrase that comes up again and again in the story of Joseph is 'The Lord was with him'.) But more often there is no moral judgement and we are left to work out for ourselves how we should respond to something a character does. (Is it right or wrong that Tamar played the role of a prostitute?) No character is wholly good – in the Bible only Jesus is portrayed in that way. And sometimes what has appeared to Christians of one century as praiseworthy seems different in a later era. (For example, slavery in these stories is not an evil; just a way of life.)

Allowing these stories to impact on our own lives is made complicated by the fact that the books were written by many authors and each had a specific reason for writing. For example, the two books of Kings and the two books of Chronicles cover more or less the same period of history. Kings was written while the Jews were in exile in Babylon. The writers were coming to terms with the fact that a dreadful calamity had befallen them and trying to explain how it happened. So it recounts the failures of the kings of both the northern kingdom (Israel) and the southern kingdom (Judah). However, Chronicles was written later, after the Jews had returned to the Promised Land. The writers of that book wanted to boost people's confidence in the religious leaders who were urging them to put their trust in God. So, in their retelling of the story, the northern kingdom is hardly mentioned and they clean up the stories of the kings of the Jews.

To give an example, in the book of Kings, Manasseh was a despicable ruler of Judah who 'filled the streets of Jerusalem with innocent blood', but in Chronicles he is brought low and calls out in repentance because he 'knew that the LORD is God'. To prove his change of heart he took the idols of worthless gods out of the Temple and destroyed them. It would have been immensely encouraging to the first readers of Chronicles to know that, beyond disobedience and trauma, there was a way back to God.

Now, let's be frank! There are some stories in the Old Testament that you wish were not true, but they are. The Hebrew tribes were typical of people in the Bronze Age. Violence figured in their lives a great deal. From the perspective of the twenty-first century we long for God's people to be distinct from those who worshipped non-existent gods, but they made war as ferociously as anyone else. For many readers of the Bible this is a huge problem, so it gets a chapter of its own in this book. That chapter won't solve the problem of all the bloodshed in the Old Testament, but at least it won't duck the question.

And while we're on the subject, here's another admission. There are some stories in the Old Testament that you wish were true, but they're not. Historians and archaeologists today question many aspects of the Bible's account. (A talking donkey, anyone? Treat yourself to Numbers 22.)

The versions of the stories we now have in the Bible were edited together 500 years or more later. There may have been written versions before then, of course, but there were no journalists interviewing the eyewitnesses, and five passing centuries can have a distorting impact on the way a story is told. Of course, it's possible that events in the history of the Jewish people took place precisely as they are portrayed, but the evidence from other sources, such as ancient manuscripts or archaeological digs, just isn't there.

For example, the Vast And Mighty Kingdom Of David, which is spoken of with awe five centuries later, might not have been so extensive or powerful as it seems. Archaeology has shown that Jerusalem was much smaller than you imagine a capital city to be. Where manuscripts other than the Bible show kings of surrounding countries establishing complex systems of government, David had a volunteer army and a following that was mainly his family. Theologians tend to think that the accounts of David's life written 500 years later are so triumphant because they date from that dreadful period when the Jews were in exile in Babylon and they needed a hero to keep them united and determined to return to their homeland.

There are three ways in which people react to this. Some people seek to fit the stories together so that they can maintain a belief that every word is true. Some people lose confidence in the Bible so completely that they refuse to let it have an impact on their lives at all. Some people are happy to accept that accounts from such a long time ago are always unreliable but focus on the overarching truth, which is that God's people looked back at their history and saw his hand in them being the occupiers of the beautiful land in which they lived. Only you can decide which one you find satisfying.

BARE NECESSITIES!

The history of the Jews and how they came to dwell in the land where Jesus lived and died is told in 12 chunky books. Choosing a dozen verses to represent all that is not so much bare necessity as barefaced cheek. This passage is set at a time when, under the leadership of a man called Joshua, the Hebrew people had conquered Canaan, the region that they saw as their Promised Land. The book it comes from is named after Joshua, and the reference is 23.1–11.

It's impossible to date accurately the events it describes, but if it was a question in a pub quiz and you answered 1200 BC you'd probably get a point. Joshua and Judges are, unfortunately, books in which it is impossible to be sure that events happened in the way described. They may have done, but there's no evidence from other sources against which to test them.

The Bible portrays many of these events as miraculous. For example, in the first battle against the Canaanite people, the fortifications of the city of Jericho disintegrated when the Hebrews sounded trumpets and shouted words in praise of God. (It is described in the song: 'Joshua fit de battle of Jericho, and de walls came tumblin' down.') In reality it was probably more mundane. Archaeology shows that Jericho had been uninhabited for five centuries, so the Hebrews may have just occupied it rather than demolishing it.

There are two things that will be helpful for you to know. First, the Hebrew people called themselves 'Israel'. It means something like 'grappling with God'. But when you come across the word in the Bible it doesn't mean the same as the state of Israel that has been a nation in the Middle East since 1948. An awful lot changed during the centuries between. So statements made about Israel in the Old Testament are not meant to be read as statements about citizens of Israel today.

Second, you will see that sometimes the word LORD is written in capitals. It refers to God, obviously, but it's that special name for God, YHWH, which was mystically revealed to Moses, the great leader of the Hebrews. This name is picked out in capitals because it became very precious to the Hebrews, reminding them of God's utter commitment to them. Here is a piece from Joshua 23.1–11:

> After a long time had passed and the LORD had given Israel rest from all their enemies around them, Joshua, by then old and well advanced in years, summoned all Israel – their elders, leaders, judges and officials – and said to them: 'I am very old and well advanced in years. You yourselves have seen everything the LORD your God has done to all these nations

for your sake; it was the LORD your God who fought for you. Remember how I have allotted as an inheritance for your tribes all the land of the nations that remain – the nations I conquered – between the Jordan and the Great Sea in the west. The LORD your God himself will push them out for your sake. He will drive them out before you, and you will take possession of their land, as the LORD your God promised you.

'Be very strong; be careful to obey all that is written in the Book of the Law of Moses, without turning aside to the right or to the left. Do not associate with these nations that remain among you; do not invoke the names of their gods or swear by them. You must not serve them or bow down to them. But you are to hold fast to the LORD your God, as you have until now.

'The LORD has driven out before you great and powerful nations; to this day no one has been able to withstand you. One of you routs a thousand, because the LORD your God fights for you, just as he promised. So be very careful to love the LORD your God.'

The Promised Land was small. It was less than one-tenth of the size of the UK, but it was fertile, excellent for mining and very desirable. It was impressed on God's people that the great privilege of living in that place brought with it great responsibilities.

What do you sense is the implication for believers regarding how the privilege of experiencing God's love should shape their lives today?

BARELY MORE!

To understand why it was so significant for the Hebrew people to have a home of their own, read some of their back story. They had been slaves in Egypt. They regarded their liberation from slavery, under the leader Moses, to be the defining moment in their history. They called this the exodus (meaning 'going out'), and a book of the Bible is named after it.

Moses was himself a Hebrew, but when he was a baby he was adopted by one of the Pharaoh's family and brought up in the palace. As a young adult he became increasingly aware of his heritage, and an awe-inspiring encounter with God left him burning with a sense that he must strive to end the brutality that the Hebrews were suffering. He used his access to the Pharaoh to plead on their behalf. When that failed, a series of increasingly devastating calamities overtook the Egyptian people. Spend half an hour reading in Exodus 11—14 how it climaxed and the dramatic escape that followed.

The rest of the book of Exodus sees an entire generation of Hebrew people eke out an existence as desert nomads. It was during this time that the famous Ten Commandments became the moral foundation of the lives of God's people.

Here's something to look out for as you read the story of the exodus from Egypt. A feature of the New Testament is that many of the ideas in it which are important to Christians echo events recorded in the Old Testament many centuries before. It is as though God has a plan that has criss-crossed time. Events in Hebrew history that gave people an insight into the ways of God seem to come to fulfilment in the life and work of Jesus. Let us think about some of these next.

Jesus spoke the truth to those who perpetrated injustice. Do you see that passion for justice foreshadowed in this story?

For Christians, eating and drinking together has a profound significance – it forms the basis of Communion (or Eucharist or Mass). Can you see its roots?

Christians describe commitment to God as a kind of freedom. Where might that idea come from?

Where is the origin of someone or something dying so that people can be saved from death? (Incidentally, one of the names given by the first Christians to Jesus was the Lamb of God.)

In Christian baptism (or christening), passing through water symbolically marks a new start as God's own. Might that have its origin in these stories too?

UNCOVERED!

Many of the characters in these Old Testament books are known because their stories have been told in Hollywood movies or children's books. If any of these names are familiar to you, these are the places where you can read their original stories.

- *Abraham* (who is regarded as the founder of Judaism, and also revered in Islam as an ancestor of Muhammad): Genesis 12—25.
- *Joseph* (who rescued not only his family but also a nation under threat of famine): Genesis 37—50.
- *Moses* (who led God's people out of slavery): Exodus 1—40.

- *Samson* and *Delilah* (a warrior of extraordinary strength and the woman who laid him low): Judges 13—16.
- *Ruth* (a refugee who thrived as a result of quick wits and kindness): Ruth 1—4.
- *David* (who rose from obscurity to become the most significant king in Jewish history, both godly and deeply flawed): 1 Samuel 16—31 and 2 Samuel 1—24 (including highlights such as the legendary duel with the giant Goliath in 1 Samuel 17, and lowlights such as his adulterous affair with Bathsheba in 2 Samuel 11).
- *Solomon* (David's heir, famously wise until wealth and sex in eye-popping quantities turned his head): 1 Kings 1—11.
- *Elijah* (who roared and raged to draw people's attention to God, but at personal cost): 1 Kings 17—21 and 2 Kings 1—2.
- *Zedekiah* (the last of a series of dismal kings, under whom Jerusalem was conquered): 2 Chronicles 36.
- *Daniel* (who was thrown to lions for refusing to renounce faith in God): Daniel 1—6.
- *Esther* (who had guts as well as beauty and overcame a genocidal plot against the Jews): Esther 1—10.
- *Nehemiah* (who led the Jews back to the Promised Land and rebuilt Jerusalem): Nehemiah 1—6.

8 Laws and lives

There are about 600 rules in the Old Testament, which the Hebrews were expected to obey in order to demonstrate their faithfulness to God. They stretch from Exodus to Deuteronomy in the Old Testament, and mark the point at which most people who try to read the Bible from beginning to end give up.

For Christians these rules have always provoked uncertainty. Some of them seem to demand timeless obedience:

You shall not murder.

Others are blatantly disobeyed in the twenty-first century, such as this one, which just seems baffling to anyone with a bit of Lycra in their cotton pants:

Do not wear clothing woven of two kinds of material.

Because rules that are universal and others that are obscure are side by side in the pages of the Bible, Christians who want to love and follow Jesus ask themselves, 'Do I need to obey them all? Do I need to obey any of them? If some, why not others?' (Those two, incidentally, are Exodus 20.13 and Leviticus 19.19.)

Exodus, Leviticus, Numbers and Deuteronomy are presented in the Bible as if they were written during the 40 years between the Hebrew people escaping their slavery in Egypt and taking the Promised Land by force. These were their 'wilderness years'. In fact the books were edited into the version we read in the Old Testament many centuries later. Deuteronomy was probably written in the seventh century BC, when a young, reforming king named Josiah was ruling Judah. It seems likely that the other three were composed 100 years or more later after the Jews had been conquered and taken into exile.

It is highly likely that parts of them were in existence for many years before that. Some would have been written down. Some would have been memorized and passed from father to child through the generations. And ten commands that were considered of supreme importance were chiselled on stone. More than anything else, these have shaped the world view of the Christian and Jewish faiths. They include laws about how humans should relate to God, for instance:

You shall have no other gods before me.

and there are others about how humans should relate to each other:

You shall not commit adultery.

For hundreds of years (although less so today) the 'Ten Commandments' were read out in church as part of weekly worship. They appear to be ageless and irrefutable. You can find them in Exodus 20.1–17. However, even these apparently timeless rules have some elements that begin to make you think, 'Times have changed. So does this still apply?' For example, the final commandment includes the words:

You shall not covet your neighbour's wife.

There is no mention of coveting you neighbour's husband because a wife is being regarded here as part of a man's property. Although it was typical of the culture of the time, it is absolutely not the way Christians think of marriage – not in the first century and not in the twenty-first century.

So if even the Ten Commandments need to be reconsidered carefully in our very different culture, what should we do about all the other rules, such as the law that forbids eating pork or (more controversially) the law that forbids homosexual practices?

The most helpful way to think about the Old Testament is to go back to the beginning of this book and remind yourself what 'testament' means. It means 'covenant'. Through this old covenant God and humans were bound together. They would be his people; he would be their God. It was a contract. In return for the incalculable blessing of being loved, protected and favoured by God, the Hebrew people had obligations to keep these laws.

The coming of Jesus changed everything. There is a New Testament. This is the covenant under which Christians live. It is a new contract, under which following Jesus is met with freedom, forgiveness and grace. For Christians, a relationship with God is not dependent on obeying 600 rules, but on opening themselves to his love, which has been expressed most fully and generously in Jesus.

Christians follow Jesus. They don't have a relationship with God that is dictated by rules or achievements; they do have a relationship that is driven by love. When Jesus was asked about the laws of the Old Testament, he picked out two as all-important (Mark 12.30):

'Love the Lord your God with all your heart and with all
your soul and with all your mind and with all your strength ...
Love your neighbour as yourself. There is no commandment
greater than these.'

Christians look for a way of honouring the purpose of the Old
Testament laws without being shackled by them. That involves
the exegesis (context) and hermeneutics (interpretation) that are
now familiar.

Some of the laws were about how God was to be worshipped
in the Tabernacle – the beautifully ornamented tent that was the
focus of the Hebrews' dedication to the Lord. Here is one (Leviticus
14.19–20):

The priest is to sacrifice the sin offering and make atonement
for the one to be cleansed from their uncleanness. After that,
the priest shall slaughter the burnt offering and offer it
on the altar, together with the grain offering, and make
atonement for them, and they will be clean.

This would be impossible to obey, because the Tabernacle no
longer exists. Because of everything that Jesus has done, however,
Christians rejoice in the fact that it has been superseded. The
death and resurrection of Jesus have brought forgiveness not just
for an individual but for all people in all times and places. The
law speaks to the twenty-first century of the importance of God's
forgiveness in our lives, but it is not a law that binds Christians.

Other laws were there to ensure that people had integrity
in an age before police or lawyers. Does Leviticus 5.1 remind you
of anything you might hear in a courtroom today? 'If anyone sins
because they do not speak up when they hear a public charge to

testify regarding something they have seen or learned about, they will be held responsible.'

The age has passed in which a religious leader would gather the community around him and shout about the need for information concerning a crime. However, today is definitely an age of workers spending sleepless nights wondering whether to become whistleblowers, newspapers knowingly printing untrue information, and people summoning the courage to speak of seeing a powerful person harass a woman or someone from a minority group. Across the centuries, this verse makes it clear that God is on the side of those who speak the truth.

Among these laws to prosper the well-being of those living in the Bronze Age were some concerning foods that had a tendency to cause ill health. That's why shellfish and pork were forbidden. These were not rules randomly inflicted to deny joy to the Hebrews.

Other rules that seem irrelevant to a mechanized age also speak to us once their original intention is clear: 'Do not muzzle an ox while it is treading out the grain.' The muzzled ox of Deuteronomy 25.4 could not eat the corn. That meant a farmer could gain every last grain of profit, but it destroyed an exhausted animal. Anyone working on a zero-hours contract will take heart from the fact that the Christian God has always had his heart set against employers who seek profit at the expense of those whom they use, whether that's an ox or a packer in a warehouse.

There are also obscure regulations, such as not sowing two different crops in one field or weaving two materials into one garment. These were more significant for what they stood for than for their impact on life. There were and are some things that just don't mix. That applied to farming and to clothing. But those were merely visual aids to remind the people of God of the really important issue: worship of the true God could never be mixed with praying to idols. These rules were and are about single-mindedness in the way faith is expressed.

Because it cannot be avoided any longer, how are we to deal with Leviticus 20.13? 'If a man lies with a man as one lies with a woman, both of them have done what is detestable. They must be put to death.' In truth, there isn't agreement among Christians about how to give full respect to the fact that this rule is one of the 600. Even following the careful process that has been outlined in order to work out how the Old Testament laws speak to the present day, the conclusion has deeply divided people who revere the Bible equally highly.

Some Christians would categorize this law as a fundamental part of God's intention for humankind. They would place it alongside the unchangeable commands such as the ones denouncing theft. They point out that the New Testament repeats the assertion that homosexuality is something shameful, associating it with idol worship. In many parts of the Christian world this is vigorously asserted.

Other Christians group this rule among those that were designed for the well-being of a generation long gone. They point out that our understanding of the science and psychology of homosexuality has transformed across the centuries. They would say that the rule should be considered in the same light as others based on limited understanding, such those that stigmatize women at certain stages of their menstrual cycle. On that basis a committed gay relationship is as honourable as one between a man and a woman.

The two sides have argued so stridently that it would be possible to conclude this is the most important rule anywhere in the Bible. It isn't. But it illustrates that using the laws of the Old Testament wisely is not straightforward. They cannot be slapped thoughtlessly across the twenty-first century. (If we did, we would have to start imprisoning people with tattoos.) And yet they are part of the Bible and their purpose has to be acknowledged. (If we didn't, lying under oath would become something we shrug off.)

The rules were given so that the Hebrews would have a good and happy life, not to make them miserable. That longing of God for people to live their lives to the full has not changed in the age of Netflix and Facebook.

BARE NECESSITIES!

From hundreds of regulations that made up the legal framework of the Hebrew people, and later the Jews, here is a group chosen more or less at random. They are taken from Exodus 23.1–9.

The first few seem to be ageless. Similar principles are lodged in UK law today. A couple that relate to farm animals appear at first glance to be obsolete today, but there is nevertheless something important about animal welfare and the way we respond to those we do not like that ought to guide our behaviour in our very different circumstances. And the final one is once again so topical that we read it with shame:

> Do not spread false reports. Do not help the wicked by being a malicious witness.
>
> Do not follow the crowd in doing wrong. When you give testimony in a lawsuit, do not pervert justice by siding with the crowd, and do not show favouritism to a poor person in a lawsuit.

If you come across your enemy's ox or donkey wandering off, be sure to return it. If you see the donkey of someone who hates you fallen down under its load, do not leave it there; be sure you help your enemy with it.

Do not deny justice to your poor people in their lawsuits. Have nothing to do with a false charge and do not put an innocent or honest person to death, for I will not acquit the guilty.

Do not accept a bribe, for a bribe blinds those who see and twists the words of the innocent.

Do not oppress an alien; you yourselves know how it feels to be aliens, because you were aliens in Egypt.

These rules suggest that Hebrew leaders faced four temptations in their legal system: fake news, befriending crooks and then being coerced into committing perjury, kow-towing to influential people, and institutional racism. Most readers of this book don't spend their days in law courts, but there are equivalent everyday temptations: spicy gossip, settling for inadequate standards because everyone else does, deferring to those who might be useful in the future, or blaming society's problems on foreigners. Is anything in these age-old words connecting with your life?

BARELY MORE!

Read Deuteronomy chapters 14—16. You will find regulations about what food would keep families healthy in the desert, 'tithes' that paid for religious and civic life like an income tax, laws that reduced the inequalities between rich and poor people, and instructions about how God should be worshipped. If you find yourself thinking that these laws are unexpectedly helpful and level-headed, go on to read chapter 17, which is more extreme and problematic.

As you read these chapters, ponder the following.

Go through the process described in Chapter 2 of this book that helps these ancient words speak to today's circumstances. First, what would these rules mean to those for whom they were originally written? Then and only then, what might be written today in order for that original intention to convey meaning to our very different circumstances?

UNCOVERED!

For a longer look at the Hebrews' legal system, I suggest Deuteronomy chapters 4—25. This section of the Old Testament starts with a command to the Hebrews to remember that they were completely dependent on God. It ends with a command never to forget. Among the laws, you will find the story of how the Ten Commandments were given and the splendid tale of a golden calf, showing how easy it was for the Hebrews to turn to idol worship when God stopped doing what they wanted. It's a *Star Wars*-length read, but you may need to add in time for bewilderment and possibly outrage.

9 The violent bits

Violence is commonplace in the Bible. There is no way of ignoring that fact. It's true, of course, that violence dominated daily life for anyone who lived during the Bronze Age. Every document of every civilization in that era was written in a context of brutality, but that's no comfort. Christians proclaim that worshipping Jesus leads to peace. There is an expectation that the Bible will show the way of peace being preferable to the way of war. We want the Old Testament to be different from the other documents of its time. It isn't.

The history of God's people includes battles in which the Hebrews ferociously conquered the tribes who lived in the land that they believed God had chosen for them to occupy. They in turn were brutalized. God is repeatedly said to demand that his followers should wipe out those who worship other gods – men, women and children.

In the New Testament, the story of Jesus and the first Christian church is in many ways a contrast. Jesus taught his followers to oppose in non-violent ways the regime that oppressed them. When he himself was tortured he responded with words of forgiveness. Jesus memorably told his followers to love their enemies and pray for those who persecuted them. However, even among the words of peace that have shaped the Christian world view there are unsettling statements.

People who do not believe in God find this extremely disturbing. They use it as evidence to suggest that religion has always been something that propels people towards war.

However, Christians are equally troubled. Even though thousands of years have gone by, they worship the same God who once ordered his people to slaughter their enemies. There is no fully satisfying explanation for why the God who is endlessly merciful should appear to condone violence.

The First World War marked a turning point in the way Christians thought about warfare. The scale of what humankind endured was unprecedented. Soul-searching led theologians of that generation to see parallels between the carnage and the events described in the Old Testament. Three ways of trying to make sense of the violent bits of the Bible emerged, and 100 years later they are still being discussed.

The first way of thinking asks Christians to consider what true evil is really like. Maybe there are some evils that are so great that only annihilation can deal with them. This suggestion emerged again after the Second World War, when the use of atomic bombs in Japan brought hostilities to an end, but at a horrifying cost. It is true that the religion of the Canaanite people who were wiped out by the Hebrews involved despicable practices such as the sacrifice of children and ritual prostitution. Was this perhaps an evil that was so intolerable that only extreme violence could end it?

There are real problems with this way of thinking, though. The Hebrew people were themselves persistently fallible and immoral. It's hard to see how a God who is completely just would want innocent children to be killed so that a new group of sinful people could take their place.

The fact that the coming of Jesus has changed everything is a second way of coming to terms with the bloodshed of the Old Testament. More fully than any book or any person, Jesus has shown the world what God is like. The God who is described in the Old Testament demands that when evil is immense it must be confronted by an army, but the God who is described in the New Testament demands:

> Do not repay anyone evil for evil. Be careful to do what is right in the eyes of everyone. If it is possible, as far as it depends on you, live at peace with everyone. Do not take revenge, my dear friends.

These words come from Romans 12.17–19. Did God perhaps change as a result of the resurrection of Jesus?

This way of thinking is problematic too, though. The distinction between the two halves of the Bible is not as pronounced as it first seems, because the Old Testament is also crammed with words attributed to God that overflow with mercy and love. The idea that God was totally different after Jesus died and rose again was first suggested by a theologian from Turkey called Marcion in the second century. Was it welcomed as a brilliant insight? Well, he was excommunicated and called a shameless blasphemer. Does that answer your question?

A third suggestion is that although God hasn't changed since time began, the way people understand him has. The writers of the Old Testament were only human. They didn't have magical insights that allowed them to think in the way people would come to think many centuries later. So when the Hebrews were victorious in battle, the writers interpreted it as God's reward for worshipping him. By the time Christians were writing the New Testament, however, they had encountered Jesus and been transformed by his teaching. It had allowed them to grasp what God wants for the world in a much more accurate way than those who chronicled the Old Testament. Jesus changed their way of thinking about war and about God.

This viewpoint doesn't make any single atrocity in the Bible easier to bear. But it does allow you to see the whole, overarching narrative of the Bible as a painful, stumbling progress from a primitive belief that God demands bloodshed to the belief that God is abounding in love and rejects violence. For the first three centuries after the New Testament was written, Christians were, almost without exception, pacifist.

BARE NECESSITIES!

I feel rather uncomfortable choosing a Bible passage for you to read just because it's violent. This is a story about Elijah. It's a rattling good story, but there's a distressing twist that doesn't usually get mentioned. It comes from 1 Kings 18.20–40.

Elijah was a prophet – a man or woman charged with making people understand God's perspective on events. He lived in Israel in the ninth century BC. That's several generations after the golden age of King David. The kingdom had split into south and north, and the north (where this took place) had a succession of lousy kings.

For centuries afterwards, Elijah was revered by the Jews as a towering figure. In fact his name is still mentioned every week by Jewish families during their Sabbath worship. He was fearless in condemning kings who used their power to oppress others, or who allowed worship of the non-existent gods of neighbouring countries. King Ahab was singled out as the worst. He married a foreign queen called Jezebel, and forsook YHWH the God of Israel in favour of his wife's idol, Baal. Elijah's courage came at a cost to his mental health, because he suffered crippling depressions.

To lighten the mood of a disturbing chapter, there is something I feel obliged to tell you. When Elijah mocks the prophets because their non-existent god is doing nothing, this demure translation reads, 'Maybe he's busy.' The original Hebrew text reads, 'Maybe he's gone for a poo.'

> Ahab sent word throughout all Israel and assembled the prophets [of Baal] on Mount Carmel. Elijah went before the people and said, 'How long will you waver between two opinions? If the LORD is God, follow him; but if Baal is God, follow him.'
>
> But the people said nothing.
>
> Then Elijah said to them, 'I am the only one of the LORD's prophets left, but Baal has four hundred and fifty prophets. Get two bulls for us. Let Baal's prophets choose one for themselves, and let them cut it into pieces and put it on the wood but not set fire to it. I will prepare the other bull and put it on the wood but not set fire to it. Then you call on the name of your god, and I will call on the name of the LORD. The god who answers by fire – he is God.'
>
> Then all the people said, 'What you say is good.'
>
> Elijah said to the prophets of Baal, 'Choose one of the bulls and prepare it first, since there are so many of you. Call on the name of your god, but do not light the fire.' So they took the bull given them and prepared it.

Then they called on the name of Baal from morning till noon. 'O Baal, answer us!' they shouted. But there was no response; no one answered. And they danced around the altar they had made.

At noon Elijah began to taunt them. 'Shout louder!' he said. 'Surely he is a god! Perhaps he is deep in thought, or busy, or travelling. Maybe he is sleeping and must be awakened.' So they shouted louder and slashed themselves with swords and spears, as was their custom, until their blood flowed. Midday passed, and they continued their frantic prophesying until the time for the evening sacrifice. But there was no response, no one answered, no one paid attention.

Then Elijah said to all the people, 'Come here to me.' They came to him, and he repaired the altar of the LORD, which had been torn down. Elijah took twelve stones, one for each of the tribes descended from Jacob, to whom the word of the LORD had come, saying, 'Your name shall be Israel.' With the stones he built an altar in the name of the LORD, and he dug a trench around it large enough to hold two seahs of seed. He arranged the wood, cut the bull into pieces and laid it on the wood. Then he said to them, 'Fill four large jars with water and pour it on the offering and on the wood.'

'Do it again,' he said, and they did it again.

'Do it a third time,' he ordered, and they did it the third time. The water ran down around the altar and even filled the trench.

At the time of sacrifice, the prophet Elijah stepped forward and prayed: 'O LORD, the God of Abraham, Isaac and Israel, let it be known today that you are God in Israel and that I am your servant and have done all these things at your command. Answer me, O LORD, answer me, so these people will know that you, O LORD, are God, and that you are turning their hearts back again.'

Then the fire of the LORD fell and burned up the sacrifice, the wood, the stones and the soil, and also licked up the water in the trench.

When all the people saw this, they fell prostrate and cried, 'The LORD – he is God! The LORD – he is God!'

Then Elijah commanded them, 'Seize the prophets of Baal. Don't let anyone get away!' They seized them, and Elijah had them brought down to the Kishon Valley and slaughtered there.

This tale is often read to children in churches, but storytellers stop before the final paragraph. What is gained and lost by doing that? Is honesty about these stories always preferable?

BARELY MORE!

If you have half an hour to spare, read the whole story of King Ahab. You'll find it in 1 Kings 16.29—22.40. There is a great deal of slaughter in this narrative, right through to his own grizzly end.

Several things are unsettling. God does not stop the atrocities, and on some occasions people clearly see themselves as pleasing God with the violence they commit. And yet there are some surprises.

In the midst of the brutality and Elijah's depression, the way God reveals himself most clearly is through 'a gentle whisper'. (A hymn writer in the nineteenth century memorably called it 'a still, small voice of calm'.) What do you feel this adds to our understanding of God and violence?

Another incident also puts the bloodshed in context. Poor Naboth was killed because a tyrannical leader coveted a lush piece of land that he owned. But on this occasion God was shown to be unequivocally on the side of justice for those who are oppressed. Does that diminish the awfulness of the violence or just make it more problematic in other places?

UNCOVERED!

Read an entire book of the Bible that is both joyful in the triumph of good and perplexing in its gory conclusion. The book of Esther will take about an hour to read (or in sporting terms, the length of a netball match). She was a Jew who lived during the low point in their history when Jerusalem had been overrun and its people taken captive to Babylon (Persia). A woman of great courage, she succeeded in saving the Jewish people from a massacre, but the account does not end there. Their revenge is shocking.

10 Songs and sayings

There are 65 books in the Bible that Christians regard, in one way or another, as God's message to humankind. But there is another one that seems different. That is the book of Psalms. These are the heartfelt messages of men and women to God. Sometimes their messages are charged with joy; sometimes with pain or doubt, but every one of the 150 songs in the book is pumped with honesty.

About a third of the Old Testament is written in poetry. The poetry of the Bible is typical of Hebrew verse of the time. It has lines in pairs, but they don't rhyme. The second line echoes the first in its rhythm or content – it might have a variation on its imagery, or develop the meaning, or answer back. Occasionally the composer uses a technical device that doesn't translate very well into English, such as having the first letter of each line work its way through the Hebrew alphabet. The beginning of Psalm 27 is typical and typically jubilant:

> The LORD is my light and my salvation –
> whom shall I fear?
> The LORD is the stronghold of my life –
> of whom shall I be afraid?

The psalms were composed to be accompanied by music. In Christian and Jewish worship they still are, sometimes chanted and sometimes rearranged into a song (often a sweeter version than the raw original).

They were written over the course of many centuries, but during the fifth century BC, when the Jews returned from exile and began to rebuild the Temple in Jerusalem, they were brought together as a cycle. Some of them specify the instruments for which they were composed – strings or pipes, for instance. Some of them are associated with particular musicians. Nearly half of them are headed 'David's psalm'. That might mean they were commissioned by him, dedicated to him or even composed by him. No one knows.

Every sentiment that an honest person might need to express to God is here in the psalms. As a hymn book, the collection is a great deal more far-reaching than those used in Christian churches today. Some are joyous, but some are utterly bleak.

Many of the psalms were and are sung in praise of God. They acclaim his power or love, declare the wonder of the world in which we live, or acknowledge God's protection as centuries have unfolded. They thank him with all the gladness of life at its best. The beginning of Psalm 8, for instance, gains in poetic intensity as centuries go by and new astronomical discoveries unfold:

> O LORD, our Lord,
> how majestic is your name in all the earth!
> You have set your glory above the heavens.
> From the lips of children and infants
> you have ordained praise

> because of your enemies,
> to silence the foe and the avenger.
> When I consider your heavens,
> the work of your fingers,
> the moon and the stars,
> which you have set in place,
> what are mere mortals that you are mindful of them,
> human beings that you care for them?

However, the largest group of psalms is completely different. These songs concern themselves with doubt and despair. Many lament that the tender closeness of God that the writer once experienced is gone. Prayers are now met with an empty silence. Some people who read the Bible for the first time expecting to find propaganda about how good God is are taken by surprise to find yearning such as this in Psalm 88:

> I cry to you for help, O LORD;
> in the morning my prayer comes before you.
> Why, O LORD, do you reject me
> and hide your face from me?

Some of these psalms work their way through depression and loneliness to find a way back to hope that God will once again be a source of help. But this one ends in the kind of desolation that many people living with mental ill health recognize:

> You have taken my companions and loved ones from me;
> the darkness is my closest friend.

In contrast, there are psalms that speak of the settled contentment that comes when you conclude that you are loved by a good God. Some of these portray God as a mother. While God is so inexpressibly greater than all human concepts of gender that neither 'he' nor 'she' is really appropriate, translations of the Bible usually opt for male language. (So does this book, for which I should perhaps apologise.) When we are asked in Psalm 131 to picture God as female, its rareness makes it all the richer:

> My heart is not proud, O LORD,
> my eyes are not haughty;
> I do not concern myself with great matters
> or things too wonderful for me.
> But I have stilled and quietened my soul,
> like a weaned child with its mother;
> like a weaned child is my soul within me.

A fourth theme, which is more troubling, is vengeance. Several psalms plead with God to defeat the enemies of the Jews. They sometimes use graphic language. For instance, the people of Zion (the hill on which Jerusalem was built) had been tortured, raped and transported into exile. They were taunted by their conquerors and forced to sing for their entertainment. I suspect Psalm 137 was not the kind of entertainment the Babylonians had in mind:

> By the rivers of Babylon we sat and wept
> when we remembered Zion.
> There on the poplars we hung our harps,
> for there our captors asked us for songs,
> our tormentors demanded songs of joy;
> they said, 'Sing us one of the songs of Zion!' . . .
> O Daughter of Babylon, doomed to destruction,
> happy are those who repay you for what you have done
>   to us –

those who seize your infants
and dash them against the rocks.

In all its variety, this book of the Bible is one that is not there just to be read, but to be used. It provides exhilarating words of praise for Christians to use together in worship. It allows men and women who are living with depression to find a place in God's presence that they can occupy with honesty. And, rightly or wrongly, plenty of Christians see acts of terrorism reported on the news and secretly pray for God to destroy those who have been responsible for doing evil. The worshippers of the fifth century BC didn't keep those thoughts secret, but brought them into church. It was a lack of taste or a lack of hypocrisy, depending on your point of view.

The poetry of the Bible (like all great poetry) approaches the great themes of life and death in a way that opens them up in an exploratory sense, rather than closing them down into statements of fact. Those who want to be told what to believe find them the hardest part of the Bible. However, those who want to dwell on the most important issues of human existence glimpse out of the corner of their eye ideas that make them wonder.

Some of the Bible's poetry is about whether it is possible to believe in a loving God when the world is riddled with suffering. The book of Job tells the ancient story of a man who refused to abandon his faith despite all the misfortune that life threw at him. At the heart of it is a long discussion of why a world created by a good God contains so much anguish. It's presented like a stage play in verse, with right and wrong ideas in dialogue until finally the voice of God himself thunders in.

Song of Songs is an erotic poem. It describes a romance between a man and a woman. Other characters appear giving advice, warning against underage sex and providing aphrodisiacs. Meanwhile the lovers intimately describe each other's beauty as part of their foreplay. Phwoar! At some points in history the poem has been interpreted as being about the love of God for his people. To be honest, that sits very awkwardly with the sexy bits. The bare Bible doesn't get any barer.

The book of Proverbs is partly poetry. It also has hundreds of memorable couplets which stand alone. It's a collection of sayings of Israel's wise men and women. They were a recognized group of people who were trusted for turning godliness into practical action. The way they gave their advice was as maxims, jokes and riddles. Proverbs is an anthology of them. They give advice on friendship, business, health, money, shopping and relationships. The sayings are very practical. They were designed to make sure that people didn't end up with an admirable spiritual life but lonely, callous, addicted or, worst of all, skint.

Along with some of the other poetic books of the Old Testament, this kind of writing is called wisdom literature. In the first chapters of Proverbs, Wisdom is personified as a fine (but rather prim) woman. The first priority for a successful life is to have reverence for God, and then Wisdom will be the best possible guide through life if you get to know her.

So how do you get wisdom? The answers are stretched into memorable exaggerations. Sleeping with someone you are not married to will burn you alive (either with shame or with an STI). Idleness is catastrophic. ('The sluggard' is a memorable character – he's so lethargic that he can get his hand into a dish of food, but he's too lazy to get it up to his mouth.) Drugs are a direct route to poverty. All these failings characterize a life of folly. (If you want to see the wit with which this advice is expressed, look at Proverbs 5.3–4; 19.24; 23.30–35.)

Obeying your parents, though, is likely to be more sensible. Friendship is life's most precious gift. Seeking justice for people who are destitute will bring blessing to poor and rich alike. And you can never go wrong if you respect the authorities. (See the whip-crack sayings in Proverbs 30.17; 18.24; 14.31; 24.21–22.)

The reason Proverbs is still a vital book for those who want to use the Bible to shape their world view is that every verse stabs us with a reminder that the Christian faith has an impact on what we do from Monday to Saturday, as well as what we do on Sunday. The way of Jesus demands integrity in everyday, mundane life. The message of the book would be easier to apply to the twenty-first century if the proverbs mentioned cannabis, payday loans and Tinder, but they are no less powerful because they refer to wine, pledges and dark alleys.

BARE NECESSITIES!

Psalm 42 is the bleak song of someone in the grip of dejection. The singer compares himself to an emaciated deer scraping its carcass through the desert dustbowl. God has abandoned him. It almost certainly dates from the period when the Jews had been conquered and many taken into exile in Babylon.

It's one of a dozen psalms attributed to the Sons of Korah, a family who had historically been associated with music in the tent for worship known as the Tabernacle. It looks back to days when leading the worship of God in Jerusalem was a joy. Now not only is the singer in a foreign land among people who mock

his religion but also at the very time he most needs God's re-
assurance, all he hears is silence. He experiences a moment's relief
on Mount Mizar. He has a vision of water cascading over him
and it's a brief insight into God's love. But at the end of the psalm
he is back where he began – desolate and trying not to lose hope
altogether:

> As the deer pants for streams of water,
> so my soul pants for you, O God.
> My soul thirsts for God, for the living God.
> When can I go and meet with God?
> My tears have been my food day and night,
> while people say to me all day long, 'Where is your God?'
> These things I remember as I pour out my soul:
> how I used to go with the multitude,
> leading the procession to the house of God
> with shouts of joy and thanksgiving among the festive throng.
> Why are you downcast, O my soul?
> Why so disturbed within me?
> Put your hope in God, for I will yet praise him,
> my Saviour and my God.
> My soul is downcast within me;
> therefore I will remember you from the land of the Jordan,
> the heights of Hermon – from Mount Mizar.
> Deep calls to deep in the roar of your waterfalls;
> all your waves and breakers have swept over me.
> By day the LORD directs his love,
> at night his song is with me – a prayer to the God of my life.
> I say to God my Rock, 'Why have you forgotten me?
> Why must I go about mourning, oppressed by the enemy?'
> My bones suffer mortal agony as my foes taunt me,
> saying to me all day long, 'Where is your God?'

Why are you downcast, O my soul?
Why so disturbed within me?
Put your hope in God, for I will yet praise him,
my Saviour and my God.

It's not unusual for Christians to experience times when God seems silent or remote. What does it add to the Bible that these feelings are acknowledged in it?

BARELY MORE!

To get a sense of the purpose of the book of Proverbs, read chapter 1. Then read chapters 22 and 23 for examples of the humour, practical advice and concern for justice that are marks of the book.

These are enjoyable reading, but are they still wisdom in the twenty-first century? (Before you rush to say 'Yes', read again the ones about smacking children. Before you rush to say 'No', consider the ones about what it feels like to be poor.)

UNCOVERED!

The intriguing poem called Ecclesiastes gives an unexpectedly sympathetic hearing to the idea that food, drink, sex and sun are all you need on God's good earth. It includes the words of a cynic that we are supposed to read and reject. In response to them are the ideas of someone who has reflected deeply on God's eternal values. Sometimes it's difficult to tell which is which, but it ends with the clear warning that there is a God who will bring all we do to judgement in time, or beyond time. Reading it is an hour's worth of richly poetic pleasure.

11 Prophecies and judgements

A prophet is a man or woman who speaks on behalf of God to the generation in which he or she lives. Not a fortune teller. Not a psychic who sees the future. A prophet is someone who announces: 'My fellow human beings, I have examined the actions of this generation and immersed myself in the ways of God, so I'm going to be frank with you about what the consequences of what you are doing will be.'

There are scores of prophets mentioned in the Old Testament. Elijah was one of them – we last met him a couple of chapters ago roaring God's condemnation of those who worshipped the god Baal. He anticipated that this would be a doorway to doom. He was correct. Another was a woman called Huldah. One of the kings of Judah sought her advice over the authenticity of a scroll containing what is now part of the Old Testament. Just 16 of them, all men, had their writings collected in the Bible. (There is a book called Lamentations in the middle of them, which contains five poems saturated with grief about the destruction of Jerusalem.)

The 16 all lived between the middle of the eighth century BC and the middle of the fifth century BC. Those were years of political turmoil, during which there was flagrant unfaithfulness to God and disregard of his laws. Perhaps a written record was required so that generations to come could look at those particular centuries from God's viewpoint – warnings and encouragements.

As previous chapters have shown, those three centuries were scarred by civil war and loss. In 750 BC the northern kingdom, Israel (sometimes called Ephraim by the prophets) was characterized by injustice against the poor and the vulnerable. Amos and Hosea were writing at that time. The message was that as far as God was concerned, Israel was no better than any of the godless nations that surrounded it, and as a result would be obliterated. The northern kingdom was conquered by Assyria in 722 BC.

Subsequently, the subject of many of the prophets was the sinfulness of the southern kingdom, Judah. Another superpower, Babylon, was rising and the threat it posed was the subject of Jeremiah, Joel, Micah, Nahum, Habakkuk, Zephaniah and Obadiah (although it's difficult to date the last one).

Judah was defeated and many of its inhabitants dragged into exile in 587 BC. From the misery of Babylon, the prophets who wrote of the return and restoration of God's people were Ezekiel, Haggai, Zechariah and Malachi. The long book of Isaiah is unusual in that it has at least two authors, and it was written partly before the catastrophe and partly during the exile.

Jonah and Daniel stand out because their prophecies are delivered in the setting of mythological stories. They are wonderful stories and crammed with meaning, but different in style from, say, Amos. He was a shepherd who got himself an education but still wrote with the down-to-earth imagery that a farmer would use. In contrast, Jonah is presented to us as a reluctant prophet, thrown overboard from a ship on which he was travelling in the opposite direction from where God had called him to go. He was swallowed by a gigantic fish, which took him to the place where God intended him to deliver a prophetic call to repentance. Daniel is portrayed as a zealous prophet, courageously defying a ban on prayer to God. He was thrown into a pit of lions, from which he emerged unscathed. He then received a series of mystical visions in which God's people endure a period of great suffering before a kingdom of joy and righteousness is established.

To understand the purpose of the prophets you need to remind yourself about the covenant between YHWH and the Hebrew people. The covenant (or testament, as in the Old . . . you're ahead of me) defined the bond between God and those who worshipped him. In a sense, the prophets were go-betweens responsible for enforcing this covenant, which had been stated over and over again. It was crucial to the call of Abraham, whose descendants were to be faithful to God and only to him. It was reiterated in the leadership of Moses – the laws of the first five books of the Bible spelled out how faithfulness to the covenant should be demonstrated. Under David too the covenant was reaffirmed, with the promise that his descendants would be honoured by God for ever. In the myths of Noah and of Adam the promises of God, and the responsibilities that accompanied them, were even more far reaching and took in all of humanity.

The message of the prophets was that a good, just and almighty God was in control, and always would be no matter how woefully his people and their leaders behaved. He had been faithful to his promises under the covenant. However, Israel and Judah had played their part in that glorious bond of love and faithfulness lamentably.

The prophets pleaded with people to put their trust in God, and implored their leaders not to forge international alliances because that would involve compromising and acknowledging non-existent foreign gods. In a sense the prophets could indeed see into the future, since they anticipated catastrophes during the coming few years that would be the logical consequences of the people being ungodly.

One of the accusations that still resonates is that God's people had failed to provide justice for the most vulnerable members of their community. They were castigated for exploiting the poor and not protecting those who were unable to make a living for themselves. God would judge them severely for this by allowing their enemies to defeat them.

Sometimes the prophets wrote furiously and sometimes tenderly. Alongside their messages of outrage came words of hope that it was never too late to repent and seek God's forgiveness. Here, for instance, are words from the very beginning of Isaiah addressed to the people of Judah:

> Ah, sinful nation,
> a people loaded with guilt,
> a brood of evildoers,
> children given to corruption!
> They have forsaken the LORD;
> they have spurned the Holy One of Israel
> and turned their backs on him . . .
> Your hands are full of blood;
> wash and make yourselves clean.
> Take your evil deeds out of my sight!
> Stop doing wrong, learn to do right!
> Seek justice, encourage the oppressed.

> Defend the cause of the fatherless;
> plead the case of the widow.
> 'Come now, let us reason together,' says the LORD.
> 'Though your sins are like scarlet,
> they shall be as white as snow;
> though they are red as crimson,
> they shall be like wool.'

Among the warnings of defeat in battle, all of which came to pass, the prophets spoke repeatedly of God's longing to be a Saviour to his people. In the books that were written during the years when the Jews were in exile in Babylon, there was a growing expectation that God would cause a new leader to rise who would restore the Jewish people by creating a kingdom marked by justice and love. This leader was distinguished with the description 'the Anointed One'.

Anointing was not a new phenomenon — kings, priests and prophets themselves were anointed as a sign of the specialness of their role. So it is not always clear to whom the Bible refers, but increasingly a single, unique figure was anticipated. For Christians the significance of this is made evident when the Hebrew form of the word 'anointed' is used: 'Messiah'. And it becomes even clearer when translated into Greek: 'Christ'.

It is tempting to suppose that every line of the prophets' writing is about the coming of Jesus Christ. In fact only about 2 per cent of the prophetic books concerns the Messiah. The vast majority concerns the politics of the time in which they were written. Even when lines cry out to be seen as foretelling the life of Jesus, most are not. For instance, when Isaiah writes that 'kings will bow down before you' he is referring to the city of Jerusalem 500 years before Jesus, not a famous manger in Bethlehem.

However, there are places where the Anointed One described by Isaiah definitely anticipates the coming of Jesus. We know without doubt that this is one of them because Jesus himself read it out in a synagogue in Nazareth, probably in AD 26, and announced that it was about him. It describes the life and work of Jesus superbly. However, even here Isaiah meant it first to be understood as referring to Zion (the hill on which Jerusalem stood) in his own century. It begins chapter 61:

> The Spirit of the Sovereign LORD is on me,
> because the LORD has anointed me
> to preach good news to the poor.
> He has sent me to bind up the broken-hearted,
> to proclaim freedom for the captives
> and release from darkness for the prisoners,
> to proclaim the year of the LORD's favour
> and the day of vengeance of our God,
> to comfort all who mourn,
> and provide for those who grieve in Zion –
> to bestow on them a crown of beauty instead of ashes,
> the oil of gladness instead of mourning,
> and a garment of praise instead of a spirit of despair.

Most of the writings of the prophets are in poetry, with its familiar pairs of lines that don't rhyme but belong together. However, some of the books also contain narratives that describe incidents from the lives of the writers. Often the prophets acted out in dramatic ways the warnings they were giving.

The most extreme of these was Hosea. He offered his entire heartbreaking relationship as a message from God to Israel. He married a woman called Gomer, knowing that she would find it impossible to stay faithful to him. She abandoned her children and slept around as a prostitute, but Hosea was so desperately in love that he paid for her to come back and spend time with him. The yearning poetry that accompanies this shows the marriage as a picture of God's love for his people. They were unfaithful to him in the idols they worshipped and the alliances they formed, but such was God's loving-kindness that he could not let them go. (You can read this in the first three chapters of Hosea.)

A hundred and fifty years later in Judah, Jeremiah bought new pants, wore them and then buried them behind some rocks. When he dug up the ruined remains some time later, presumably in front of a disgusted audience, he declared that God's intention had been to stay as close to the Jewish tribes as underwear is to a body. The faithless people had fouled the relationship (chapter 13, if you don't believe me).

It is, to be honest, difficult to read the 16 prophetic books without help. It's straightforward to work out the mood – judgement, tenderness, pleading or cursing – but to work out what nation and what century is referred to in each chapter requires a commentary. If you are just trying to uncover the bare Bible, it won't really repay the effort.

However, it might help to take a 'Doctor Who' approach, which allows you to think about the words of the prophets in four time zones. By far the most important zone is the century for which the message was originally written. Don't be distracted from that. Even events that the prophets anticipated as happening in the future, such as defeats in battle, are now in our very distant past.

A second zone is the time of the Messiah. Although the prophets were the enforcers of the Old Covenant and its laws, some of the writings look forward to a New Covenant. Christians look at words such as 'the year of the Lord's favour', with its promise of freedom, comfort and good news for the poor, and unmistakeably see the person of Jesus Christ.

A third time zone is our anticipated future. Jesus spoke of the day when God will bring earthly time to a close. He will establish a kingdom in which poverty ends, the oppressed find justice, and the sick are permanently healed. The life of Jesus has given Christians additional information that the prophets never had. His vision of the future means that their words still inspire us, even if it is in ways they never intended.

The fourth time zone is our own. I say that cautiously, because these are not prophecies that can be casually dropped into the twenty-first century as if they had a magic meaning. But if you read Isaiah's marching orders, 'Seek justice, defend the oppressed', and think that only past generations needed to be told that, you haven't been paying attention.

BARE NECESSITIES!

Amos 8.1–8 starts with a joke. The prophets attribute a lot of puns to God, but the humour is as black as pitch. Then there is a shockingly violent warning of what is to come. The poem seems to be a satirical song describing people who are fed up with religious festivals because for 24 hours they have to be good before they can romp back into corruption. Then God's judgement is chilling:

> This is what the Sovereign LORD showed me: a basket of ripe fruit. 'What do you see, Amos?' he asked.
>
> 'A basket of ripe fruit,' I answered.
>
> Then the LORD said to me, 'The time is ripe for my people Israel; I will spare them no longer.

'In that day,' declares the Sovereign LORD, 'the songs in the temple will turn to wailing. Many, many bodies – flung everywhere! Silence!'

Hear this, you who trample the needy and do away with the poor of the land, saying,

'When will the New Moon be over
that we may sell grain,
and the Sabbath be ended
that we may market wheat?' –
skimping the measure, boosting the price
and cheating with dishonest scales,
buying the poor with silver
and the needy for a pair of sandals,
selling even the sweepings with the wheat.

The LORD has sworn by himself, the Pride of Jacob: 'I will never forget anything they have done. Will not the land tremble for this, and all who live in it mourn?'

About 28 centuries have gone by, but is there anything about the economics of the nation or the globe today that might benefit from hearing the distant echo of these words? We know that the devastation that befell Amos' country was the logical outcome of their behaviour. Am I alone in finding this uncomfortable reading?

BARELY MORE!

Try Isaiah chapters 52–55. These beautiful poems come from the time of the exile in Babylon. They give new hope to a people on the verge of despair. A key character is the one whom God describes as 'my Servant'. He is dreadfully abused but restored to become the hope not just of the Jews but of the entire world. Perhaps this is the Jewish nation. Or perhaps it is the coming Messiah.

In churches, Isaiah 53 is very often read during the days that lead up to Easter. Can you identify ideas in it that encourage Christians to recognize something about Jesus' death and resurrection?

UNCOVERED!

Reading a sizeable chunk of one of the prophets is hard work. Especially if you hit an indigestible tirade against an obscure nation. So I've chosen a part that has a variety of styles, but is mainly a narrative. It's Jeremiah 27.1—40.6.

This section is easier to read because it's set in a specific time and place. The place is Jerusalem, which had been besieged by King Nebuchadnezzar. When the city finally fell, its finest young people were taken captive and transported to Babylon. Nebuchadnezzar installed a puppet king who would oversee what was left of Jerusalem as long as he handed over vast sums of money and did what he was told. The hapless king was called Zedekiah.

Jeremiah was the prophet who brought God's perspective on events. Zedekiah chose to ignore Jeremiah and made some disastrous decisions, such as seeking an alliance with Egypt. The result was that Babylon lost patience and razed Jerusalem to the ground. Zedekiah's fate was truly horrible, and you will find out when you read it whether or not Jeremiah survived.

There are several reasons why it's worth a couple of hours of your time. It begins with an acted-out prophecy. Jeremiah straps on a yoke of the kind that would be used to force oxen to do what a farmer wants. The implication is that this is Jerusalem's fate. Interestingly, a rival prophet called Hananiah gives a completely different, crowd-pleasing message. He declares that God will change everything miraculously and Jerusalem will revert to the good old days. This makes him extremely popular, but he is proved wrong.

There follows a poetic prophecy in which God reveals that the fall of Jerusalem will be terrible, but that God's people will find Babylon to be a place where they can not only survive but also thrive. They will, after several generations have passed, be restored.

Jeremiah's prophecies were unpopular, but true. The rest of the narrative shows him paying a price for his honesty, but not in the way you might expect.

12 Extraordinary visions

The sixty-sixth dimension. Away from any time and place we recognize. They do things differently here. We are going to visit the book of Revelation and some other parts of the Bible that are haunted by mysterious visions.

The style of literature you find in Revelation is called apocalyptic. People find it intriguing, but they don't know what to make of it. The letters that immediately precede it towards the end of the Bible are factual and practical. Suddenly the landscape changes to dragon-infested pits over which fly trumpet-playing angels. They are as different as a wildlife documentary and a fantasy movie. On twenty-first century television we appreciate both. The problem with Revelation is that the world has forgotten how to appreciate once-familiar literature of this kind. So it's like turning on the TV expecting a programme about chickens hatching and instead seeing vampires pushing open a coffin lid.

Apocalyptic writing was always a feature of a time of persecution and suffering, of which there was a great deal in the centuries during which the Bible was written. It contained dreams of grotesque creatures (but no vampires – they came 18 centuries later). The dreams were always presented as if they were dredging up hoary secrets from antiquity with cryptic meanings. The message was invariably that beyond these days of anguish would be a future of peace and justice. In some ways this is like the work of the prophets. However, the Old Testament prophets tended to use more down-to-earth images and call wayward people back to God. Apocalyptic imagery is bombastic, but it's always leading towards hope for those who stay faithful.

The author of Revelation gives his name as John. He's not likely to have been the John who was Jesus' friend because it was written at the very end of the first century. He tells us that he is writing on the Greek island called Patmos, and that he is there as a result of suffering. It's possible that he fled the persecution of Christians by the Roman Emperor Domitian. There is certainly a great deal of violence in the book, in which he tells his readers about a fantastical vision of the future that God revealed to him one Sunday. But the purpose of the book is to make it clear that the destiny of our troubled world is the permanent establishment of peace and righteousness when God triumphs.

It begins with John seeing a vision of Jesus, blazingly magnificent. The name used for Jesus is the Son of Man. It's a name Jesus used of himself, according to the Gospels. He took it from the Old Testament book called Daniel, where it's associated with a future time when God will bring the universe as we know it to an end and make himself known gloriously to the whole world. ('A son of man' is also used in the Bible to mean 'ordinary bloke', so it evokes Jesus as both human and divine.)

Then there are seven letters. They are written to churches, like others in the New Testament. However, they use more extravagant metaphors and each one follows the same pattern. They are critical (for instance, of wishy-washy Christians), but inspirational for dark times (Revelation 3.8): 'See, I have placed before you an open door that no one can shut.'

After the letters, spectacular scenes unfold. A throne appears on which God takes his place. Extraordinary creatures worship him. A Lamb enters who is alive but once was dead, and is acclaimed as the only one who is truly worthy. (This is obviously meant to make us think of Jesus.) The seals that lock up a vast scroll are opened, unleashing world-changing events such as wars and earthquakes. A great multitude of humans who have stayed faithful to the salvation that Jesus brings come into God's presence with rejoicing.

Trumpets sound, heralding plagues and environmental catastrophes. A pregnant woman, a beast, a seven-headed dragon and (later) a carousing prostitute appear, but after a ferocious war the angel Michael casts the dragon out of heaven. Bowls brimming with miseries of various kinds are tipped over the earth, wreaking destruction and leading to a climactic battle. Babylon, the code name for all that is evil in the world, is destroyed.

A colossal multitude of people worship God. The Lamb prepares for marriage and a banquet is spread. After a trial, the beast is cast into a lake of fire and the dragon is imprisoned. Jesus Christ and those who have been martyred because of their faith in him reign for a thousand years. Then the dragon gets free and makes war against God's people, but is defeated. After a show trial, God pronounces judgement and the dragon is thrust into the lake of fire alongside Death itself and all who have done evil.

A glorious new heaven and new earth appear. Suffering and sadness are brought to an end conclusively by God, who makes his home among his people for ever. A tree of life grows, whose leaves heal the nations and abolish evil. In a joyous finale, Jesus promises to return to earth and fulfil the hopes of all who long for an end to injustice.

And . . . breathe!

It is a sensational journey. Along the way we encounter names that have found their way into films and fantasies: the four horsemen of the apocalypse, the number of the beast, the Antichrist, the battle of Armageddon, and the New Jerusalem.

There are also numbers that have deep significance. Many things come in sevens, which seems to imply their perfect completeness. The number 666 famously represents evil (if you change the letters of the name of the vile Emperor Nero into their equivalent numbers and add them up, that is the sum).

The number 1,000 signifies immensity, and 12 is a reminder both of the number of tribes of Israel in the Old Testament and the number of Jesus' disciples in the New Testament. So a crowd of 144,000 worshippers of God is . . . well, do the maths and draw your own conclusion.

So what on earth are we to make of the Revelation to John?

The first thing to be aware of is that it is not as unique in the Bible as it first seems. Apocalyptic literature was, in its time, familiar. Daniel, written about 200 years before Jesus but set several centuries before that, has similar visions of beasts, battles and a Son of Man who would come on clouds to be worshipped by all. And the dream of a decisive Day of the Lord in which all that is wrong would be put right comes in many Old Testament prophets. The original readers would not have found it as strange as we do.

Strange? Well yes! So much so that there are several different methods that Christians have used in order to make sense of it.

First, there is a view that has seen the images of Revelation as representing events in the whole sweep of human history from the first century to the present day. So the tribulations unleashed in the early chapters symbolize the vicious persecutions experienced by Christians during the century after Jesus. So many tyrants (and I'm afraid to say, popes) have been identified as the Antichrist that picking out any one would seem unreasonable. In every single century, the triumphant return of Jesus ('the Second Coming') has been expected imminently. And the seven letters have been taken to stand for succeeding generations of the church, always ending with the unflattering assumption that Revelation 3.16 refers to the present day: 'You are lukewarm . . . and I am about to spit you out of my mouth.'

An alternative way of thinking about Revelation is that the images, even though they were projected into the future, all stood for events that had already taken place by the time the book was written. So the great tribulation is a metaphor for the siege and destruction of Jerusalem in AD 70, a terrifying period during which tens of thousands of Jews and Christians died. The prostitute and the beast she rides are metaphors for Rome and its tyrannical empire. And so on.

There are further ways of looking at the apocalyptic sections of the Bible. Some anticipate the events as literal incidents that will overtake humankind on a day yet to come. There are several variants of this interpretation that focus on the period of a thousand years during which the followers of Jesus will reign with him while those who reject him are 'left behind'.

Others suggest that attempting to associate the flamboyant images with actual events, whether past, present or future, misses the point. Rather, Revelation should be seen as a kind of allegory of the spiritual path on which all Christians travel, struggling as good and evil exist side by side in the world. For instance, it is possible to see the dragon as a symbol for the relentless wickedness of a system in which the poor are trapped in poverty by the rich.

So that gives you four different ways of interpreting Revelation. Each way of thinking has a very, very long title, and I can't bring myself to inflict those on you. The main reason for spelling them out is that some interpreters of the Bible become dogmatic about particular ways of approaching these wonder-filled chapters. People write books about why their interpretation must be right and everyone else's is wrong. However, it is always worth remembering that no matter what interpretation you read someone else has a different, but just as sincerely thought-out, point of view.

BARE NECESSITIES!

The Bible climaxes with a vision of God and humankind reconciled and eternally at peace. It's an explicit statement that death is not the end. There is no detail of any kind regarding what humans can expect to experience after their lives on earth are over, but there is a rich and positive painting of the mood. These words are from Revelation 21.1–6.

> Then I saw a new heaven and a new earth, for the first heaven and the first earth had passed away, and there was no longer any sea. I saw the Holy City, the new Jerusalem, coming down out of heaven from God, prepared as a bride beautifully dressed for her husband. And I heard a loud voice from the throne saying, 'Now the dwelling of God is with human beings, and he will live with them. They will be his people, and God himself will be with them and be their

God. He will wipe every tear from their eyes. There will be no more death or mourning or crying or pain, for the old order of things has passed away.'

He who was seated on the throne said, 'I am making everything new!' Then he said, 'Write this down, for these words are trustworthy and true.'

He said to me: 'It is done. I am the Alpha and the Omega, the Beginning and the End. To those who are thirsty I will give water without cost from the spring of the water of life.'

We don't know what heaven will look like. (If you have concluded that it will look like a load of buildings dressed in a wedding frock, you've missed the point.) But we do have an inkling of what it will feel like: a bit like the operation was successful and you're not hurting any more; a bit like waking up and knowing it's your wedding day; a bit like finding a waterfall when dying of thirst seemed the only possibility; a bit like you've mastered the alphabet and unlimited knowledge has opened up (alpha and omega are the first and last Greek letters).

Humans seem hardwired to want to know what lies beyond death. The Bible says very little, but it is relentlessly positive that the followers of Jesus will find it perfect. Is that sufficient?

BARELY MORE!

You're going to want to read the Book of Revelation. I know you are. There are 22 chapters, which begin bizarre and swell until they break the weirdometer. If you absolutely can't resist, pick a few random chapters! You'll find images that encourage you to think that you're beginning to make sense of it. (For instance, there's an earthquake in the face of which warmongers, corrupt billionaires and tyrants whimper because they know it's God's judgement – that's chapter 6.) You'll find others that are utterly obscure. (For instance, there are two witnesses who can breathe fire and turn water to blood – they're in chapter 11.) In between, you will find hymns of praise to Jesus that are marvellously uplifting and that have sustained Christians when they have been fed to lions, beheaded or bombed, but discovered that such terror has not changed their conviction that Jesus is their God. (Enjoy chapter 7.)

However, I am going to make a plea. Don't google 'What does Revelation mean?' You'll find hundreds of websites written by men and women who have devoted their lives to providing a specific interpretation for every event described. They will tell you they have no doubt that a particular world leader, alive or recent, is the Beast of whom John wrote all those years ago. Or that a specific political event is the upturned Bowl of Wrath. It is quite possible that they will explain how they've worked out from the numbers in the book precisely the day on which the world will end. (And it will probably be next Friday, leaving you fretting about what to do with the holiday tickets you bought for Saturday.) This has been done scores of times and it has always been wrong.

Just ignore all that. Throughout the Christian centuries certain people have rejected a measured reading that allows this book to keep its secrets, and instead forced its images to mean something about the years and the nations in which they themselves live. Time has proved one interpretation after another to be mistaken.

Many online interpretations of Revelation are outlandish and scary, but the book itself, although it is honest about the fact that terrible things happen in this world, ends with permanent peace and healing. That is what the followers of Jesus should take from it.

So if you can possibly resist the allure of those sensational chapters, may I suggest that instead of reading Revelation . . .

UNCOVERED!

Read a parable of Jesus. It comes in Matthew 25.31–46. It too is set at the end of earthly time. Like most of Jesus' stories, the Bible itself will not tell you what to make of it. You must decide what it means, but here's a clue – it isn't literally about sheep and goats.

The reason I am suggesting this is because it reveals important things about the ultimate destiny of humankind, but it takes your attention away from warriors with eyes of blazing fire and instead makes you ask yourself what you are doing here and now for the poor, hungry and oppressed.

13 How the Bible came to be written

Why did Jesus never write a book? I've no idea! Perhaps he would have done if he had lived to 60, but he died aged 33. This means that God's clearest communication with human beings is not through a book (no matter how much Christians value the Bible) but through a person.

Jesus was an educated man. In fact, the only story in the four Gospels from his adolescence is about how his brain impressed the Temple priests, but he surrounded himself with people who weren't like that. The people who established the very first churches were fishermen or tradesmen. They must have been bright because they ran businesses, but they weren't scholars. Some churches were hosted by women, who would only have had an education if they were wealthy. All of them, whether or not they were literate, knew chunks of the Old Testament by heart.

Twenty years after Jesus, something new happened. Intellectuals began coming to faith and sharing the leadership of Christian communities. There was Paul, from the university town of Tarsus in Turkey. He went to Jerusalem to study under Gamaliel, a Jewish rabbi who taught a broad range of philosophy and ethics. Elsewhere, the New Testament speaks of a leader called Apollos, who was from Alexandria in Egypt (also a university town) and saturated in knowledge of the Old Testament.

So what was the version of the Old Testament they were reading? It hadn't been written as a complete book from beginning to end, like a novel. By the time of Jesus, parts of it had existed for a long time. A few of the psalms had been sung for a thousand years by the time Jesus sang them. Deuteronomy seems to have existed as a book (or rather, as a scroll) by the seventh century before Jesus. The Bible describes the Ten Commandments being engraved on tablets of stone. That would have been during the fourteenth century BC. The language is similar to other texts from that period that have survived on stone, so it's not far-fetched.

However, most of the Old Testament was written and the existing parts edited during the sixth century BC. That's the period during which the Jewish people were captive in Babylon. If you look back at Chapter 7 you will remember what a bleak time that was for the Jews. There was a real danger that they would be absorbed into their enemy's population and culture, and that their religion would just dissolve into Babylonian ways. Scribes and historians set to work to create a record of all that God had done so that the Jews would never lose their sense of identity. Tradition has it that Ezra wrote these books. (I love a good tradition, but I suggest you treat this in the same way as the tradition that Robin Hood robbed from the rich to give to the poor.)

The first five books of the Old Testament came to belong together and were revered as a crucial part of Jewish life by about 400 BC. That's Genesis, Exodus, Leviticus, Numbers and Deuteronomy. Together they are known by several names – the Law, the Torah, the Pentateuch or the Books of Moses. Moses was traditionally held to be the author. (The Sherriff of Nottingham, the Merry Men . . . you get the picture!)

Alongside the Law were the works that were explored in Chapter 11 of this book – the Prophets. (In the Jewish Bible, though, the books we know as Joshua, Judges, Kings and Samuel were included and known as the Former Prophets.) These were validated as part of Scripture in about 200 BC.

The third collection of books was called the Writings. That was accepted as part of Scripture (or 'the canon') about 100 years before Jesus. It consists of the Psalms, Proverbs, Job and the rest of the Old Testament.

Now it gets complicated. There is a group of books that is included in some Bibles but not others. For hundreds of years it was not certain which books were in the canon of the Old Testament and which were not. So some Bibles are bigger than others. There are 66 books that everyone agrees on. The next chapter explores another group known as the Apocrypha, which some editions of the Bible add.

In the third century BC the Jews, who were conquered by one empire after another, were under the control of the Ptolemy family who ruled a kingdom whose capital was in what we would now call Egypt. During this time a translation of what we now call the Old Testament was made from Hebrew to Greek. Tradition has it that it was commissioned by King Ptolemy II himself. (Maid Marion, Friar Tuck, Little John!)

The translation was known as the Septuagint. That means 'the seventy', because that's the number of Jewish experts who worked on it. Sometimes it is referred to as LXX, which is 70 in Roman numerals. They began with the Law – the first five books of the Bible. As the process continued and the Prophets and Writings became widely acknowledged as part of the canon, the scope increased until all of our Old Testament, plus the Apocrypha, was included. That is the Bible Jesus and all the writers of the New Testament read – we know that because they quoted from it.

Ironically, the Old Testament that Jesus read was not the one that Jews subsequently came to view as the most reliable version. Between the eighth and tenth centuries AD, Jewish leaders established a definitive version of their Scriptures in Hebrew. It was known as the Masoretic text (the Masoretes were scholars in the Middle East). It contains the 39 books of the Old Testament, but not the Apocrypha. It was compiled with great attention to accuracy. To make sure that every handwritten copy was exactly the same, the Masorete copiers would count the number of letters from the beginning of a book and the number of letters from the end. If the middle letter of the copy was the same, they knew it was accurate. (Although I'm sure their passion for detail was driven by godly fervour, it's also true that copiers were paid per letter, so there was another incentive for all that counting as well.)

And the New Testament? Our Bibles contain 27 books, which were written between 20 and 70 years after the life of Jesus. Other books about him were also written during those years. Most are lost, but it's still possible to read some of them. (There is more about them in the next chapter.) Deciding which ones were the canon of the New Testament was a gradual process. The letters of Paul were held in high regard from an early stage. By the end of the first century they had been copied many times and were circulating as a collection.

In about AD 130 a bishop called Marcion drew up a list of the books he considered should be in the Bible. He was a controversial figure though. He excluded the entire Old Testament from his list because he thought the God described there couldn't possibly be the same God who sent Jesus. He was eventually thrown out of the Church altogether. That's what prompted Christian leaders to define which books should be regarded as inspired by God.

Various councils of Christian leaders met to discuss this over the next two centuries. There is a letter by a very significant Egyptian bishop called Athanasius dated 367 in which the 27 books we are familiar with are listed together for the first time. Then a council of Christian leaders from around the world met in Carthage, North Africa, and the decision was sealed. That was in 397, about 400 years after the birth of Jesus.

About that time an Italian man called Jerome, who'd been a bit of a naughty boy as a student, had a very serious illness. When he recovered he made up his mind that he was going to devote the rest of his life to Jesus. He wrote dozens of books, but his most significant achievement was translating practically the whole Bible into Latin. Latin was a language that could be read throughout what was then thought to be the entire world. (Of course it was only a fraction of the yet-to-be-explored globe.) He was the major contributor to the version of the Bible that would be recognized by the Church as the standard text for hundreds of years – the Vulgate.

At the risk of annoying the 90 per cent of the world's population who don't speak it as their first language, I thought you might like to know how the Bible came to be translated into English. When Christians began to come in some numbers to what is now the United Kingdom, the handwritten Bibles they brought were in Latin, but from the first there was a desire to read the Bible in the local language. Manuscripts in the British

Library show translations into Old English in tiny lettering between the Latin lines of richly illustrated extracts of the Bible. Between the eighth and tenth century, sections of the Bible were translated by Bede (a monk and historian from Northumberland), Alfred the Great (king of the West Saxons) and Aelfric (a monk from Oxfordshire).

Old English (or Anglo-Saxon) is almost a foreign tongue compared with what you are reading on this page, and the language changed markedly after the Norman Conquest. Different versions of parts of the Bible continued to appear as the language developed.

The first complete Bible in English was produced at Oxford University in the fourteenth century by John Wycliffe and his assistants. He believed that the nation needed radical reform and that people needed to understand the Bible so that a new culture could be built based on its principles. However, Wycliffe had powerful political enemies who did their utmost to silence his supporters, and the result was a law shortly after his death that made it illegal to translate any part of the Bible without the permission of the church authorities.

However, within a few decades a communications revolution in Germany changed everything. With the coming of Johannes Gutenberg's printing press the ease with which the Bible could be copied was transformed. A scholar called William Tyndale was determined to produce a faithful translation of the Bible into English from the original languages. With restrictions still in force in Henry VIII's England, he had to work abroad. His English New Testaments were printed on presses in Germany and smuggled into England in bales of cloth. He was at work on the Old Testament when he was kidnapped and eventually executed. His final words, shouted from the stake, were, 'Lord, open the King of England's eyes.'

In fact, a fearsome number of people died so that you and I can read the Bible effortlessly. For centuries, allowing ordinary men and women to understand the ideas of Jesus was such a threat to those in power that they killed in order to keep the Bible remote. If you are uncovering the Bible for the first time (or the hundredth), pause for a moment to honour those whose sacrifice made it possible.

Dramatic changes known as the Reformation were underway in Europe during the sixteenth century. New churches were being founded and new attitudes to the Bible were developing. Henry VIII had declared himself Governor of the newly formed Church of England. His eyes were opened. He consented to Bibles being published in English. A version edited by Miles Coverdale, completing the work of his friend William Tyndale, was circulated.

Henry VIII went further in 1538 and commanded that a Bible in English should be placed in every parish church. Further versions followed during the reign of his daughter Elizabeth I – the Geneva Bible and the Bishops' Bible. Each was popular with different groups within the Christian Church.

James I succeeded Elizabeth. At a conference in 1604 to regulate the affairs of the Church of England it was decided that a new translation should be commissioned. About 50 scholars worked on it and it was published in 1611. This translation, the King James Version (sometimes known as the Authorised Version), has a style that is exceptionally beautiful, particularly when read aloud. For four centuries it has been loved as a great work of literature as well as revered by those who want to understand the ways of God.

Other translations of the Bible have followed. Some have taken advantage of subsequent scholarship to produce translations that are more accurate than the King James Version. Some have attempted to create versions that are simpler for succeeding generations to understand.

There were many new translations into English during the twentieth century. Titles include the Jerusalem Bible, the Revised Standard Version, the New International Version, the Good News Bible and *The Message* (not a literal translation, but an adaptation into everyday language). Most people living in the world now have a translation in their own language of at least part of the Bible. The New Testament is available in 1,442 languages, and the work of translation continues. All of them owe a debt to the King James Version, which is the world's bestselling book.

BARE NECESSITIES!

When the New Testament speaks of the Scriptures it is referring to the Old Testament. There's a cheeky occasion when one New Testament writer comments on another one. This comes from 2 Peter 3.15–16: 'Our dear bother Paul also wrote to you with the wisdom that God gave him. He writes the same way in all his letters . . . His letters contain some things that are hard to understand.'

No change there! These are some words of Paul that I would like you to read, and they are easier than most. They come from Romans 15.1–7:

> We who are strong ought to bear with the failings of the weak and not to please ourselves. Each of us should please our neighbours for their good, to build them up. For even

Christ did not please himself but, as it is written: 'The insults of those who insult you have fallen on me.' For everything that was written in the past was written to teach us, so that through the endurance taught in the Scriptures and the encouragement they provide we might have hope.

May the God who gives endurance and encouragement give you a spirit of unity among yourselves as you follow Christ Jesus, so that with one heart and mouth you may glorify the God and Father of our Lord Jesus Christ. Accept one another, then, just as Christ accepted you, in order to bring praise to God.

Endurance and encouragement – does your personal response to anything you have read in the Bible so far relate to either of those qualities?

BARELY MORE!

Read Psalm 19. The first half is about how God has made himself known in the world around us. Then the second half is about how God has revealed himself in the written word.

Keep reading. Psalm 20 is a prayer that you can use for anyone you know who is suffering in any way. Psalm 21 is a bit like the National Anthem. Psalm 22 is a searing cry of pain to a God who seems to have stopped listening. (Jesus knew this psalm by heart and shouted it as he died on the cross.)

Psalm 23 begins in the countryside, where God is a shepherd whose care for you is free range. It ends in a nightclub, where God gives you a VIP pass. Between the two you have to travel through some dark places. Psalm 24 surrenders to the supreme majesty of God. Psalm 25 allows you to ask God's forgiveness for your failings.

Which one chimes with your mood today? (Of course, it could be a different one next week.)

UNCOVERED!

The letter of James is one of the books that nearly didn't make it into the New Testament. It's missing from the oldest lists, but when the council at Carthage drew up the definitive canon it was included. Even in the sixteenth century the most significant theologian of the day, Martin Luther, huffed and puffed about it. The letter doesn't mention the death and resurrection of Jesus, so Luther dismissed it as 'an epistle of straw'.

There are six people called James in the New Testament and the author could have been any of them or someone else entirely. Tradition has it that it was the James who was Jesus' brother and leader of the church in Jerusalem, but frankly I've run out of Robin Hood gags. It is apparent, though, that it was written from a place where there was real suffering, from famine or from persecution.

It's not a long letter and you don't need to know much about history to enjoy it. It's full of challenging instructions about how to live as a follower of Jesus, especially if you live in the wealthy half of the world, and I've come to love it. As you read it, ask yourself what we would have lost if it hadn't made the cut.

14 The missing bits

There are 66 books that all Christians accept are part of the Bible. They read them as a way of inviting God to shape their lives. They stretch from Genesis to Malachi, and from Matthew to Revelation. However, it is possible that the Bible you use has 20 or so volumes in between Malachi and Matthew to which this book hasn't yet referred.

You are more likely to come across these volumes if somewhere in your family or your background you are associated with the Roman Catholic Church or the Orthodox Church. The collection is known as the Deuteronomical books. For Roman Catholic and Orthodox Christians these are as much a part of the Bible as the books described in previous chapters.

After the sixteenth century a large number of new churches were founded. They are called Protestant churches and they have names like the Church of England, the Baptist Church or the Salvation Army. If you've ever had a connection with one of these churches, your Bible probably doesn't have these books in. And the name you might have heard used to describe them is the Apocrypha. It's the name I'm going to use – it means 'hidden'.

In a part of the previous chapter that you may have skipped I introduced the Septuagint (a translation of the Old Testament from Hebrew to Greek in the third century BC) and the Masoretic text (a version of the Hebrew Old Testament established in about the ninth century AD). The Septuagint includes the Apocrypha, and Roman Catholic and Orthodox Christians use it as the basis of the Bible. The Masoretic text doesn't, and Protestants use that.

Protestant churches don't have anything bad to say about the Apocrypha, but they don't regard it as having the same authority as the Old and New Testaments. The very first Bible to be translated into English, the Geneva Bible of 1560, had a preface explaining why it included them and there hasn't been a better explanation since. It said that they are 'not received by a common consent to be read and expounded publicly in the church' but they are written by godly men and 'received to be read for the advancement and furtherance of the knowledge of history and for the instruction of godly manners'.

So here is a quick summary of what you're missing if the edition of the Bible you have does not include the Old Testament Apocrypha.

Tobit features angels and demons in a story in which righteous people are rewarded for caring for their parents, honouring marriage and marking death with reverent funerals. Through a series of extremely unusual miracles Tobit is healed of blindness and a woman called Sarah overcomes a curse and marries his son.

Judith is a Jewish double agent who defeats the enemy Assyrians single-handedly. She inveigles her way into the tent of General Holofernes, offering secret information and sex. She gets him drunk and chops his head off.

Wisdom of Solomon is addressed to those in positions of leadership. It urges them to act justly. Wisdom is personified as a powerful woman. True wisdom is not something you are born with. Only God can give it to you and he is longing to do so.

Sirach is the collected wisdom of Joshua ben Sirach, who lived two centuries before Jesus. Another name for the book is Ecclesiasticus, but because that makes it easy to confuse with the Old Testament book called Ecclesiastes, most people prefer Sirach. It's a long book, a series of poetic sayings giving instructions on how to do good. It's quite like Proverbs.

Baruch was PA to Jeremiah, the prophet whose book appears in the Old Testament. In the Apocrypha, Baruch's books reflect on the history of the Hebrew people – where it all went wrong and how the nation could even now throw itself on God's mercy. Part of it is a warning to turn from idols to God, and that part is sometimes listed separately as the Letter from Jeremiah.

Then there are three volumes that were originally part of the Old Testament book of Daniel, but were separated from it for various reasons.

The book of Azariah is prayerful. It's the song of three comrades who are sentenced to be burnt alive for refusing to renounce God. They are protected by an angel so they emerge without even being singed.

The book of Susanna is pervy. Two old men spy on a girl bathing naked and threaten to have her tried for immorality unless she has sex with them. They get their come-uppance.

Bel and the Dragon is bat-shit crazy. Daniel kills a monster by force-feeding it exploding fur-cakes. I love it! (Incidentally, bat-shit crazy is not a technical term. Theologians are more inclined to describe it as controvertible extracanonical literature.)

Maccabees recounts how, as a result of a revolt led by Judas Maccabeus and his family, the Jews overcame their enemies and established an independent state for a few golden years during the second century BC. I'll say more about that later.

Esdras contains the writings of Ezra. He was the leader who brought the Jews home to Jerusalem after many wretched decades of exile in Babylon. It includes visions of the Messiah that suggest God had turned his favour away from the Jews alone and would send his Son for the whole world's salvation.

There are also some beautiful short books such as the Prayer of Manasseh, a heartfelt confession in which the writer pleads for God's forgiveness. And there are extra chapters of familiar books.

In addition to these, there were dozens of books written in a biblical style before the time of Jesus. Their texts are still in existence, but they have never been regarded as part of the Bible. They are known as pseudepigrapha. If you've read those, you're just showing off.

As well as the books that appear in the middle of some Bibles, there are 100 or more books that form an Apocrypha to the New Testament. There are no Bibles that publish them alongside the 27 Gospels and letters which this book has been dipping into, and no churches recognize them as having the same authority as the rest of the Bible. Most of them were written much later than the books that were finally included in the list.

Some of them weren't accepted as part of the Bible because the scholars who examined them decided that their authors were twisting the sayings of Jesus to make them fit their own theories (for instance, one called the *Gospel of Marcion*). In the second century there was a lot of interest in the childhood of Jesus, because so little was known about it, and several accounts were written (such as the *Gospel of James*) that invented incidents to make it more interesting than it actually was. They didn't make the cut either.

There were also some books written about 100 years after the death and resurrection of Jesus that tried to make it more spectacular than it is in the four Gospels that were agreed to be authentic. For instance, in the *Gospel of Peter*, soldiers guarding Jesus' tomb witness two angels going into it and helping Jesus emerge. Behind them comes the cross on which Jesus died, which has gained the power to walk and talk. Yeah, right!

There are more credible books, though. In 1945 a group of ancient manuscripts was found buried at the site of a monastery in a place in Egypt called Nag Hammadi. The most well known of these is the *Gospel of Thomas*. It doesn't tell the story of Jesus, like Matthew, Mark, Luke and John, and it doesn't mention Jesus' crucifixion. Instead it's a collection of Jesus' sayings. Many of them are about the importance of love and helping the poor. Some theologians think they sound like genuine sayings of Jesus. Others think it was written long after the four Gospels we know about and the reason it sounds like Jesus is that the author had read them.

Some splendidly eccentric theories exist about these books. Hollywood movies (*Stigmata*) and best-selling novels (*The da Vinci Code*) have based their plots on schemes by church leaders to hide the fact that these manuscripts exist. The stories suggest that if the public knew about them, facts would be revealed about Jesus that would destroy his reputation. There is, apparently, a worldwide conspiracy to prevent them from being read, but when I wanted to read the New Testament Apocrypha I bought it on Amazon. If someone really is conspiring to hide it they're making a rubbish job of it.

There was never a chance that these manuscripts would be included in the Bible. Others very nearly were, however. The list of books that was considered to be part of the New Testament kept changing for several centuries. The decision over whether Revelation and Hebrews should be included was a controversial one.

There is a list of books considered to be part of the New Testament made in about 330, which includes a volume called The Shepherd of Hermas. It was written during the second century. It's a book of visions and most of them call on Christian congregations to seek forgiveness and new life. For instance, in one, the Church is pictured as a frail old lady, weighed down by the wrong things Christians do. Every time people ask Jesus to forgive them and change their ways, the woman gets younger and her grey hair regains its colour, until finally she is a beautiful bride.

The book was extremely popular, but it wasn't included in the canon when agreement was reached later that century. Another book that some Christians during those centuries thought should be included was *The Didache*. It was written in about 100, and it's a book of instructions that tells us a lot about what it was like to go to a church service in that era. From it we know how Christians were baptized, when they fasted, and how the leaders organized themselves. There are some beautiful prayers which were used when the Christians ate bread and drank wine together in the Eucharist (otherwise known as Communion or Mass). The most lasting thing that *The Didache* has given us is the Lord's Prayer. The Gospels that we read in our Bibles only have the first half. The version that is said in churches around the world, with the beautiful climax, 'Thine is the kingdom, the power and the glory for ever and ever,' comes from *The Didache*.

There is one more missing bit I would like to tell you about. The Old Testament ends with the Jews being allowed to return from Babylon to Jerusalem when an enlightened emperor called Cyrus released them. Then there is a blank page. At the beginning of the New Testament, the Jews are suffering under a different oppressor – the Romans. What happened in between?

Well, about 350 years before Jesus, Alexander the Great conquered a vast area, including the rebuilt lands in which the Jews lived. Then Alexander's empire collapsed and the Ptolemies (from the land we now call Egypt) took control. Then the Selucids (modern-day Syria) conquered them. All this time the Jews were paying their taxes to different foreign masters and yearned to be independent.

The Selucid king, a man called Antiochus, asserted his control over the Jews by taking over their Temple in Jerusalem. (A tiny part of that Temple still exists, called the Western Wall, or the Wailing Wall.) He dedicated it to Zeus and had a massive statue erected.

The Jews were incensed. Many took up arms, including two important groups. One was called the Hasidaeans, fervently religious Jews who later became known as the Pharisees. (Remember them from Chapter 3?) The other was called the Hasmonaeans, who were zealous nationalists. Their leaders were members of the Maccabees family (the ones who gave their name to books in the Apocrypha). Led by Judas Maccabaeus and his brother, they achieved military victories against the Selucids and drove them out. For a few decades, which the Jews looked back on as a golden age, they were independent.

The second century BC was not a straightforward time to be a national leader. A number of the members of the Maccabees family held power for a little while and then were either killed in battle or assassinated. And all this time, they were currying favour with an empire that was growing at a phenomenal rate to the north of them – the Romans.

In 67 BC a civil war broke out between two rival brothers in the Maccabees dynasty. Aristobulus had the upper hand for a bit, but his brother Hyrcanus had a clever mentor called Antipater, who struck a deal with Rome. He allowed the Romans to take control of the Jewish homeland if he was given the position of high priest. And that is how the Romans came to occupy Jerusalem. They didn't actually conquer the Jews; they were invited in.

Antipater died and there was another power struggle, but the Romans stamped their authority by appointing a 'King of the Jews'. He was Antipater's son and his name was Herod. You might have heard of him because he features in the Christmas story. (Not in a good way!) When Herod died, his three sons briefly succeeded him, but the Romans couldn't stomach them. So they were deposed and the Jews came under direct rule from Rome. In order to work out how much tax the Jews should pay to their new rulers a census was undertaken. (That census features in the Christmas story too.)

Governors from Rome were appointed to oversee the area, the most significant of whom in the life of Jesus would be Pontius Pilate. The governors had no interest whatever in who looked after the religious life of the Jews. So they sold the office of high priest (yes, you read that correctly . . . sold) to the highest bidder. Thus they managed to outrage every Jew of every description, including those who had been too mild to get involved up until that point.

And into that mess was born the Saviour of the world.

BARE NECESSITIES!

I have tried to choose passages that display how inspiring the Apocrypha can be, but also show it to be slightly different from the other Bible passages that have appeared at this point in each chapter. This is chapter 44 of the book called Sirach.

This is a really fine piece of poetry, and the truths in it make you reflect on history in a helpful way. But when you compare it with one of the psalms in the Old Testament that explode with praise of God, there is something a bit uncomfortable about the fact that it is written in praise of men. It makes you feel that it's on the edge of the Bible's unfolding message of salvation, not the centre of it. That is typical of the Apocrypha.

Incidentally, this extract comes from the translation of the Bible called the New Revised Standard Version. All the other extracts in this book come from the New International Version (Inclusive Language Edition), but the NIV does not include the Apocrypha:

> Let us now sing the praises of famous men,
> our ancestors in their generations.
> The Lord apportioned to them great glory,
> his majesty from the beginning.
> There were those who ruled in their kingdoms,
> and made a name for themselves by their valour;
> those who gave counsel because they were intelligent;
> those who spoke in prophetic oracles;
> those who led the people by their counsels
> and by their knowledge of the people's lore;
> they were wise in their words of instruction;
> those who composed musical tunes,
> or put verses in writing;

rich men endowed with resources,
living peacefully in their homes –
all these were honoured in their generations,
and were the pride of their times.
Some of them have left behind a name,
so that others declare their praise.
But of others there is no memory;
they have perished as though they had never existed;
they have become as though they had never been born,
they and their children after them.
But these also were godly men,
whose righteous deeds have not been forgotten;
their wealth will remain with their descendants,
and their inheritance with their children's children.
Their descendants stand by the covenants;
their children also, for their sake.
Their offspring will continue for ever,
and their glory will never be blotted out.
Their bodies are buried in peace,
but their name lives on generation after generation.
The assembly declares their wisdom,
and the congregation proclaims their praise.

I find this idea rather beautiful. When seen through God's eyes,
it is not only the famous people who stamped their name on
history who matter. Those who lived good and godly lives in
their generation, but have slipped out of everyone's memory, also
deserve to be honoured. (I would find it even more beautiful if
the poem additionally bigged up famous women, but that's how

Sirach saw the world in his generation.) Looking back on your life, who has passed through and out of it in a way that won't bother the history books but has been of enduring value to you? Spend a while honouring the memory of those men and women.

BARELY MORE!

Do you remember a king called Manasseh who got a brief mention back in Chapter 7? He was one of a line of lamentable monarchs who led the Jews away from the worship of God to idols. He is interesting because one of the two versions of his life in the Old Testament shows him coming to his senses, begging God for forgiveness and reforming his ways.

The Old Testament Apocrypha has a book called the Prayer of Manasseh. It is so powerful in acknowledging God's greatness and confessing the need for forgiveness that it is almost overwhelming.

Don't kid yourself that these were the words that King Manasseh actually used. He lived in the seventh century BC, and the prayer was written about 500 years later, but it's only a page long and reading it is a powerful experience. Lots of versions of the Bible don't include the Apocrypha, so you will need to find one that does. Failing that, the Wikipedia page for Prayer of Manasseh has the full text in seventeenth-century language.

There are some people who carry around with them the weight of something they did wrong at an earlier stage of their life. They never talk about it to anyone. However, it's there, it's a miserable memory, and their lives would be happier if they were unburdened of it. If that is you and you have some kind of belief in God, here are your words and this is the day you are set free.

UNCOVERED!

It is reasonably easy to read the books that were rejected from the final collection we know as the New Testament. You can make up your mind about whether they add to or detract from what the Bible tells us about Jesus. There are several editions. For instance, Oxford University Press publishes *The Apocryphal New Testament*, translated by J. K. Elliott. There are several other translations online.

15 How reading the Bible can shape your life

God's clearest communication with human beings is not through a book but through a person. I wrote that precise sentence two chapters ago, and then went on to something else, but it's really important. No matter how highly people of faith value the book, a Christian is not someone who follows the Bible; he or she is someone who follows Jesus Christ.

I have downplayed this piece of information for 14 chapters in case you stopped reading. The Bible is very important indeed to Christians, but the main reason it is important is that it reveals what happened at a particular time and place when God touched this planet in an extraordinary way in the person of Jesus, walking and talking among us.

The Old Testament in all its diversity tells the story of the Jewish people in the centuries before Jesus and, in retrospect, it seems to show us how the world became ready for God to intervene in that unique way. The New Testament in all its variety tells the story of Jesus, and what happened in the subsequent decades as the impact of his life, death and resurrection began to roll through the world.

Sometimes the Bible is referred to as 'the word of God' or 'the word of the Lord', but it's best to use such phrases with caution. Obviously when the Old Testament speaks of the word of the Lord it isn't referring to the whole Bible, much of which hadn't been written yet. And it also uses that phrase to describe things that didn't involve writing at all – dreams, spoken prophecies, the profound thoughts of leaders.

In the New Testament, especially in the writings associated with John, there is a very distinctive meaning attached to the word 'Word'. (It's the capital letter that gives it away.) This is how John begins his Gospel. He was attempting to answer the question, 'Who on earth is Jesus?' Although 20 centuries later he has created a problem for us because it's not easy to understand, his intention was to make everything clear for his original audience.

> In the beginning was the Word, and the Word was with God, and the Word was God. He was with God in the beginning. Through him all things were made; without him nothing was made that has been made.

Those of his readers who were Jewish recognized the idea of the Word. In their Scriptures it didn't mean 'something written down'. It meant the divine spark of God, eternally wise, endlessly creative, which had brought the whole universe as they knew it into being. Nothing could have existed without that creator, the Word.

John's readers who were not Jewish were equally familiar with the Word. (Incidentally, it is sometimes written in Greek as *Logos*.) They understood the Word to be the logic of the world, the reason that lies behind all reality. Nothing could have existed without the Word, which made the universe possible.

John writes all this about how unreachable and incomprehensible God the Word is, because he is building up to the point at which he will zap his readers with a phenomenal fact. And here it comes (John 1.14):

> The Word became flesh and made his dwelling among us.
> We have seen his glory, the glory of the One and Only Son,
> who came from the Father, full of grace and truth.

I don't need to tell you who he's talking about, do I? The unfathomable has taken on a form like you and me. There is no longer a need for your brain to be overwhelmed with the complexity of imagining what God is like. If you need to know . . . well . . . God is like Jesus.

So here's an interesting question! If that's the case, how did Jesus use the Bible? That's going to give us a helpful steer as to how we can use the Bible to improve our own lives. Fortunately, we know how Jesus used the Bible but, awkwardly, it was rather different from the way we tend to use the Bible today.

For a start, Jesus didn't own a Bible. In his day, no one did. A village like Nazareth, where Jesus lived for some time, would have had a synagogue. The synagogue would have owned a few handwritten scrolls, kept locked in a cabinet called an ark. They were extremely precious because they had been copied by hand. They would have contained parts of the prophets' writings and extracts from the history books. The most important of them were the scrolls that contained the first five books of what is now our Bible (the Torah).

On the Sabbath day the leader of the synagogue would have processed through the gathering of Jews holding the Torah. It would have been honoured joyfully because it represented the heart of the community's life. There would have been a reading from the Torah, which was specifically set for that day. Then someone else would read from other scrolls. And then there would be discussion by everyone (or rather, all the men) about what it should mean for their everyday lives.

Even in that generation there was discussion and questioning about what Scripture should mean in practice. The text they were reading referred to a specific set of circumstances, which no longer applied to them. For instance, some of the words on the scroll assumed the people were living in tents in the desert, but they were now in villages with roofs over their heads. Some of the words assumed that they were living in freedom, but they were now a conquered people. And so on. They needed to work out what lay behind the original words, and how they were going to apply them to their current context.

They had opinions and disagreements, but they worked it out together. They took the words as their starting point, and they worked out what impact they were going to have on their flesh-and-blood lives. Jesus – a highly respected leader – was one of the people who made the words become flesh, week after week.

This was usually a peaceful and positive shared experience that allowed God to shape their everyday lives and behaviour. But the reason we know they had disagreements was that one Sabbath in Nazareth Jesus was at the centre of an almighty one. If you have been reading the Bible extracts I've suggested you will remember the one I picked in the 'Barely more!' section of Chapter 2. Jesus gave his opinion that there were passages in the history scrolls that suggested that God loved non-Jews (Gentiles) as much as he loved Jews. It led to a fracas. They nearly opinion-ated the life out of him.

Why is this so important? Because from time to time today you hear someone declare, 'The Word of God says . . .' He or she then usually quotes a sentence from the Bible that appears very cut and dried. The implication is that stating this is the end of the argument. There is absolutely nothing more to talk about. For instance, 'The Word of God says that murder is a sin' is decisive (and of course, true).

The problem comes when someone uses that phrase to end an argument, but you instinctively feel that it should be the start of a conversation, not the full stop. In the time of Jesus, you could have had that conversation. Together you could have put flesh and bone on it and worked out what it means in your own lives in your own location.

Bear with me if I start with an absurd example. Suppose someone said, 'The Word of God says that there are only two ways to drink coffee – you can have it either black or white.' (There is, incidentally, no coffee in the Bible. It appears ten centuries after Jesus as a gift to the world from Muslim culture.)

In a sense, the statement that you drink coffee black or white is true. It's true enough to start a conversation, at least. You will then find yourself discussing dozens of variations, from espressos and americanos to cappuccinos and lattes, and at some point a bright spark will point out that none of these is actually coloured either black or white. The original 'black or white' statement was only useful in that it began your entertainment in the queue for your coffeehouse caffeine fix.

Now here's an example that is more significant because it's something I have actually heard Christians say in the expectation that it would bring a discussion to an end: 'The Word of God says there are only two sexes – male or female.'

In the twenty-first century we know straightforwardly that this is not correct. The Bible does indeed say something similar to that, but the facts say something different.

The reason I have chosen this example is that I have some personal experience. Thirty years ago I was asked to befriend two people whose bodies had both male and female characteristics. They were Christian people. They couldn't help being Christian, because they held beliefs deep down that they couldn't shake off that Jesus was God. They also could not help being what we now know as intersex. (The word was not in common use 30 years ago.)

Their churches found it impossible to reconcile what they read in the Bible with the determination of these two delightful and courageous people that they should be recognized as something different from either male or female. They were, to all intents and purposes, rejected.

For some reason someone suggested I was the kind of person who might be able to help. To be honest, all the help involved was meeting every couple of months and having a cup of coffee. (Of course it was always a brown colour, neither black nor white.) We chatted together about what the Bible said and how we were going to make sense of it in these circumstances. Together we tried to discover what happened when we took the words and worked them into human flesh.

We went on meeting for a couple of years, often with a lot of laughter, but occasionally with real distress. Thirty years on, it is a lot easier for people to understand and talk about intersexuality. It even has its own letter – it is the I of LGBTI. My friends have both moved abroad and over the decades Christmas cards have tailed off.

However, one of our discoveries was why those living at the time of the New Testament might not ever have come across adults who had both male and female characteristics. In the Roman Empire it was acceptable for babies who were born disabled or unwanted to be placed on a hillside by their parents and left to die ('exposed'). So intersex babies never grew up.

Christians and Jews during the first centuries after Jesus determinedly opposed this. In fact, there is a letter from Mathetes to his friend Diognetus in about 200 in which he expresses his surprise: 'Christians are no different from the rest of mankind. They do not live in cities of their own or have a different language or way of life . . . but the way they live is marvellous and confounds all expectations. They have children, but they don't kill the ones they don't want. They eat with all their neighbours, but they don't sleep with all their neighbours. They obey the existing laws, but in their own lives they surpass the laws. They love all people, even though they are persecuted by all people.'

In these days when medicine has taught us to understand human life far better than we did 30 years ago, it's hard to imagine a church today being so uncompromising in its treatment of an intersex person. However, there are other issues concerning gender and sexuality that divide churches. Some straightforwardly assert that statements in the word of God stand for all time. Others want everything that science has uncovered over the centuries to be taken into account when we decide what God wants for this generation.

The two issues that spring to mind first are whether women should be church leaders and whether same-sex couples should marry. The most confusing thing is that people with both views have a very high regard for the Bible, and yet have come to different conclusions.

We need to talk about sex! Frankly, we know a vast amount more about how life begins than the writers of the Bible did.

They knew that there was a connection between a baby being born and two people having sex nine months previously. (When you think about it, discerning that was a huge leap forward in science and our ancestors are thought to have worked it out between 12,000 and 20,000 years ago.) However, Moses and Paul (and presumably Jesus) did not know that a woman had any part to play in the creation of a baby. The best science they had access to at the time told them that when a man and a woman had intercourse, one time in every hundred a tiny but fully formed human was planted by the male into the female's womb. The only role they thought the woman had in reproduction was as a carrier for what the all-important male had generated.

There is a fair amount in the Bible about sex. Some of it makes you gasp because it seems heartless, or insulting to women or gay people. You read it and think, 'That cannot possibly be right or good in the twenty-first century.' However, everything you read in the Bible about sex, a woman's menstrual cycle, the shame of being childless, or same-sex attraction needs to be read in the light of what the writers knew (or rather didn't know) about human reproduction. The writers were doing their absolute best with the information they had available to them, but they didn't know the whole story. (Do you remember way back in Chapter 2 that I joked that I had no idea what to make of the verses about the shame a man should be plunged into if he had a wet dream? I lied to you. I knew precisely why that was considered a shocking waste. Now you do too.)

So what we need is a way to find out what God's plan is for each succeeding generation. It must take the Bible absolutely seriously, but it must also take into account everything we know that the writers didn't. We need a way of making the words of the Bible real in the lives that people actually lead, just as the Jews of Jesus' day did.

For the last 200 years we have had one.

This method, which is widely considered to be dependable throughout the Christian world, is credited to the great Christian leader John Wesley. His life pretty much spanned the eighteenth century. It would be more accurate to say that he didn't invent the method, but he popularized it. However, it's still called Wesley's Quadrilateral.

As the name suggests, Christians have four reference points when they are working out how God wants them to live.

The first is the *Bible*, of course. It gives a point of unchanging certainty about what God said and did in the world close to the time of Jesus.

The second is the *tradition* of the Church during the 2,000 years that have followed Jesus. All Christians in all times and places have together made up a body of people through whom God has unfolded his ever-developing plan. The story of the Church is no longer the account of a small, scared gathering of Jesus' followers in Jerusalem. It's the story of 20 centuries of change that culminate in the stadium-sized congregations of South Korea, the secret, forbidden clusters in Somalia who have no buildings or legal protection, and every gathering of faithful people between.

The third reference point is *reason*. Our minds matter to God and he ensured that human intelligence went on increasing after the time of Jesus. This is where all that science teaches us plays a part in showing us the mind of God for our generation. What we know about human psychology and what we seek to discover about the origins of the universe all play their part in hearing God speak.

The fourth is *experience*. What we ourselves bring to these matters is crucial because the Holy Spirit of God did not stop being active when the New Testament was written down, but is alive in our world and in our individual personalities. The story of every Christian life has its part to play in the way we meet God.

The reason I chose to write about intersex people is that it's easy to see how all four of those reference points work together to help us see the issue through God's eyes. We have the Bible and its statements about gender. We have the tradition of the Church. From the earliest days it taught that human life is of infinite value even when people have physical features that put them in a minority. We have reason. Although soon after the life of Jesus people began to recognize intersexuality (using terms we would now find unacceptable), it was only during the twentieth century that major advances in science helped us understand it. And we have experience, because the two friends I made 30 years ago helped me to realize how precious intersex people are to God not just in theory but in laughter, learning and tears.

There are very many issues that I could have chosen to write about instead, in which the Bible additionally needs tradition, reason and experience in order to guide the way we live today. I could have written about video gaming or the use of fossil fuels or cloning or the death penalty or modern slavery or drone warfare or assisted suicide or smoking tobacco or immigration. The voices of Christians need to be heard on all of these vital subjects, but none of the discussions can be brought to a conclusion by declaiming the word of God. Thinking and talking together, men and women need to recreate the word of God in living, breathing humanity. Sadly, it is not always a peaceful and loving process, as Jesus discovered in Nazareth, but with hope and with prayer, let's try!

BARE NECESSITIES!

There is a bite to this story. Jesus told it, and we have it preserved in Luke 10.25–37, but you will only feel its fangs if you add to the Bible's account things that are not immediately obvious. At first sight, it seems like a story about kindness, but actually it's a story about racism.

> An expert in the law stood up to test Jesus. 'Teacher,' he asked, 'what must I do to inherit eternal life?'
>
> 'What is written in the Law?' he replied. 'How do you read it?'
>
> He answered, '"Love the Lord your God with all your heart and with all your soul and with all your strength and with all your mind"; and, "Love your neighbour as yourself."'
>
> 'You have answered correctly,' Jesus replied. 'Do this and you will live.'
>
> But he wanted to justify himself, so he asked Jesus, 'And who is my neighbour?'
>
> In reply Jesus said: 'A man was going down from Jerusalem to Jericho, when he was attacked by robbers. They stripped him of his clothes, beat him and went away, leaving him half dead. A priest happened to be going down the same road, and when he saw the man, he passed by on the other side. So too, a Levite, when he came to the place and saw him,

passed by on the other side. But a Samaritan, as he travelled, came where the man was; and when he saw him, he took pity on him. He went to him and bandaged his wounds, pouring on oil and wine. Then he put the man on his own donkey, brought him to an inn and took care of him. The next day he took out two silver coins and gave them to the innkeeper. 'Look after him,' he said, 'and when I return, I will reimburse you for any extra expense you may have.'

'Which of these three do you think was a neighbour to the man who fell into the hands of robbers?'

The expert in the law replied, 'The one who had mercy on him.'

Jesus told him, 'Go and do likewise.'

The additional piece of information that would have made Jesus' original audience gasp, but that 2,000 years later requires explanation, is this. Two highly religious people passed by, but neither of them were willing to get involved. The guy who saved the injured man's life was someone incredibly unlikely to help a first-century Jew. He was a loathed foreigner, a traveller from despised, neighbouring Samaria. Typically, Jesus refused to explain himself fully, but he appears to be saying that someone from another religion is just as capable of showing God's love as someone who thinks that he or she has a special, exclusive relationship with him.

Wow! That is uncomfortable reading for Christians. It leaves me asking the question below.

In this decade, in this place, who is your neighbour?

BARELY MORE!

The way Paul conversed with his 'neighbours' of other faiths might interest you. Read Acts 17.1–32. First of all you see Paul among his fellow Jews in two towns on the north side of the Mediterranean Sea. The account of what happened in Thessalonica is a nail-biter because an innocent man nearly has his chips. The people in Berea are interesting because of the way they used the Bible (or rather, the Hebrew Scripture scrolls they kept in the synagogue).

When Paul gets to Athens he is no longer among Jews. He speaks to people from every other religion, or none, but he doesn't tell them, 'You've got everything wrong.' Instead he says, 'I understand the way you're thinking, and there is so much more I'd like to tell you about our world.' There are so many people in my street whom the people of Athens remind me of. This makes me want to think about the following question.

What are the 'unknown gods' that people prioritize in their lives today?

UNCOVERED!

For a longer read, I suggest the story of how the followers of Jesus grew over the course of 20 years from one small Jewish group in Jerusalem to many gatherings of Christians who had all kinds of religious backgrounds. You can find it in Acts 1—15. There's no shortage of action, with dramatic escapes, life-changing exploits and disasters that only succeed in making the story of Jesus spread.

I was tempted to stop at chapter 14, which ends in a triumph. But for the truth about the way the Christian Church grew (and still grows) you need to read chapter 15, which ends with a blazing row. God help us, Christians have never been perfect!

16 We've barely begun

This final short chapter is written in the hope that you are intrigued enough by that ancient library of books to keep going when you shut this one. I'm simply going to suggest three choices you can make. Well . . . four, if you make it to the very last sentence.

First, choose a Bible. There are dozens of English translations. Any of them is good as long as it's one that you feel enriches your life and doesn't frustrate you with language that is either too old-fashioned or too colloquial. Most translations are available as an app that you can download to a smartphone.

Every translator who works on creating a new version has already made some choices on your behalf. Every single word involves a decision as it changes from Hebrew or Greek to English. Here are a couple of the judgements a translator has already made before you open a Bible.

Jesus talked about coins and weights, but 20 centuries have gone by and our coinage and measures have changed. So the translator has to make a decision. She could write, 'The man bought some provisions costing one denarius.' That would be a literal translation, but it doesn't convey much to you and me. Or she could write, 'The man bought some provisions costing seventy pounds.' A denarius was a basic day's wage for a worker, so this translation tells us what we need to know, but it isn't precisely what the Bible originally said.

Another example? There is a Greek word *dikaios*. That word can be translated either 'just' or 'fair' or 'righteous'. So the Bible translator has to make a choice. She could write, 'God wants his people to be just' (which makes it sound like they should pursue the rights of poor people). Or she could write, 'God wants his people to be fair' (which sounds like they shouldn't cheat at sports). Or she could write, 'God wants his people to be righteous' (which sounds like they should be very devout in terms of their personal morality). They are all true, of course, but depending on which one the translator chooses, the Bible version seems a bit different.

Browse through a few Bibles in a shop or online. Google 'Bible versions and translations' and when you have skipped past the first few listings that are trying to sell you things, you will find websites that allow you to compare them all free. If you are a Shakespeare fan you might choose the ornate language of the King James Version from 400 years ago:

> Though I bestow all my goods to feed the poor, and though
> I give my body to be burned, and have not charity, it profiteth
> me nothing.

Beautiful words, but it has to be said that translations made during the last 60 years are a great deal more accurate. Some manuscripts dating from near the time of Jesus were discovered in caves in Qumran, Israel, in about 1950. They dramatically advanced what theologians know. They are called the Dead Sea Scrolls. The New

International Version in the 1970s used those advances to give an authentic translation that's easy to read with a touch of poetry:

> If I give all I possess to the poor and surrender my body to the flames, but have not love, I gain nothing.

Or you could choose a more recent version such as *The Message*, which doesn't pretend to be a literal translation, but renders the Bible into chatty, colloquial language:

> If I give everything I own to the poor and even go to the stake to be burned as a martyr, but I don't love, I've gotten nowhere. So, no matter what I say, what I believe, and what I do, I'm bankrupt without love.

(Incidentally, these are three different versions of 1 Corinthians 13.3.)

The second choice you need to make is how to get some help. There are many organizations that produce resources to help people engage with the glorious library of books we have been exploring. Let's face it, the Bible is a monster, and this book has only shown you how to cuddle up to it without it crushing you. Most people find that the best way to engage with it is by reading a short extract from it on a regular basis.

There are magazines, books and online schemes that are designed to help you get the best out of the Bible. They explain the parts that have become hard to understand because of passing time. They open up the parts that are life-enhancing and can enrich your day-to-day experience. But they also make sure that the monster is never tamed. That is important because there is so much in the Bible that is challenging to a society (or indeed a person) that has become comfortable despite knowing about world

injustice, or self-satisfied despite knowing that people in the neigh-
bourhood are struggling through life unloved.

To find out what is available, look at the websites of
WordLive, the Bible Reading Fellowship, the Bible Society,
Scripture Union, or Church House Publishing. Hunt out the
sections with titles like 'Explore', 'Reflections', 'Christian growth'
or just 'Bible'. Try out anything that's free online first. Then
invest some money in a magazine or an app that leads you on
one stage at a time.

And the third choice is to find some people to do this with.
As in Jesus' day, reading a Bible passage alongside other people
and then discussing it will reveal insights that individuals can't
find by themselves.

Many churches arrange themselves so that as well as worshipping together on a Sunday they have small groups in which
people look at Bible passages and work out what their relevance
is for everyday life. If you're not comfortable with the idea of
going to a church, find an individual who is prepared to give
reading the Bible with you a go.

Pick out a chapter from one of the Gospels or a psalm from
the Old Testament. Look at the emotions involved and discuss
whether they relate to feelings you or anyone you know have in
the twenty-first century. Ask yourself why someone all those years
ago cared so deeply about the words you are reading that he
wrote them down. Look for encouragements, challenges, hope,
guidance.

At some points, take the role of an enthusiast. There is
nothing more irritating than someone who won't even give the
Bible a chance. Talk about what captures your imagination.

At other points, take the role of an awkward codger who won't accept unsatisfactory answers. If you have a question that needs information from an expert, write it down and seek one. If you don't have access to an expert in person, take advantage of the free question-answering service provided by the Christian Enquiry Agency at their website <www.Christianity.org.uk>.

Whatever else you do with the Bible, though, attempt to treat it as a relevant book. Ancient? Of course. Read in the light of every subsequent advance in human knowledge? Of course. God's orders dictated straight into your ear? Don't be daft! It's relevant, though – even if you have to wrestle with it until the good news drops out.

BARE NECESSITIES!

This is the closest the Bible gets to explaining itself. These are the words of Paul to a young man he was coaching to take over from him. He was writing about the Old Testament, because the New Testament didn't yet exist. It's wonderful that this letter has ended up in the Bible we now have. It comes from 2 Timothy 3.14–17:

> Continue in what you have learned and have become convinced of, because you know those from whom you learned it, and how from infancy you have known the holy Scriptures, which are able to make you wise for salvation through faith in Christ Jesus. All Scripture is God-breathed and is useful for teaching, rebuking, correcting and training in righteousness, so that God's servant may be thoroughly equipped for every good work.

Those are the adjectives Paul used to describe the Bible. After what you've read for the first time (or the hundredth), what adjectives would you use?

BARELY MORE!

To understand the way Paul has shaped Christian thinking throughout the years, I would like to suggest Romans 8.1–39. Basically Paul is contrasting what life was like before Jesus (law, flesh, death) with what life is like since Jesus (the Spirit of God, the family of God, hope). The life, death and resurrection of Jesus replaced all the burdens with a relationship based on love.

Some bits of this are ferociously complicated, and you may prefer to let your eyes drift past those. Treat it like the rotating beam of a lighthouse where the darkness is suddenly overtaken by dazzling blazes of light. The bits you can understand are thrilling. Which flashes of light lift your spirits?

UNCOVERED!

If I haven't yet succeeded in enticing you into reading one of the four Gospels, this is my last chance. The one I haven't suggested yet is Matthew, so that's my choice at the end of this book.

Why have I been repeatedly suggesting you read the life of Jesus? Because about 30 years ago doing that changed me radically.

I'm from a generation that got told the story of Noah's ark as I played with the toys, and I knew the famous stories from Jesus' life because they were taught in school and church. Yet I had never read a whole Gospel like a novel or a famous person's biography.

The character of Jesus reached out and grabbed me and still hasn't let me go, although I've shaken hard enough. I am fascinated that he was brought up in the middle classes – educated, intelligent – but he turned his back on all of that and made his home among the poor. He defied convention, trod a delicate line between friends in the brothel and friends in the synagogue, inspired people that a world of justice was not only desirable but also possible, and died with words of love and forgiveness on his lips.

When they were near him, broken people found hope, suffering people experienced healing, and brutalized people glimpsed a different future. For three glorious years there was wonder in the air.

I am totally committed to living a life based on those principles. However, you then need to deal with the fact that within weeks of Jesus' time on earth, his friends were following him as their God. And because of what I've found in the Bible, I have come to do so as well.

The result has been that I've found an extraordinary sense of purpose in life. I have found things making sense that previously didn't. I think I've become a better person because I've been living for the benefit of other people instead of just myself. And most pleasing of all, I've genuinely been glad to be alive.

Skip back a page to the extract from the Bible. For me the most significant way the Bible describes itself is 'God-breathed'. Many different words could have been used to describe what God has done for the world through the Bible, but 'breathed' is the most powerful one.

Of all the objects that make up our teeming universe, which ones breathe? Living ones. That's the way to treat the Bible. Not as a dead library, but as a living one. Not as a book that has expired, but as a book that inspires. Make a decision to let God breathe into you through it. Choose life!